NATIVE ENGLISH FOR NEDERLANDERS

Ronald van de Krol

NATIVE ENGLISH FOR NEDERLANDERS

A personal, cultural and grammatical guide

Het Financieele Dagblad / *Uitgeverij* Business Contact

To Jeanet, Kate and Ayat

And with thanks to Helen Borkent for her eagle-eyed editing

Vijfde druk, januari 2008

© 2007   Ronald van de Krol
         Uitgeverij Business Contact, Amsterdam
Omslagontwerp: Het Vlakke Land, Rotterdam
Boekverzorging: LINE UP boek en media bv

ISBN   978 90 470 0050 1
D   2007/0108/325
NUR   801, 610
       www.businesscontact.nl
       www.fd.nl

Foreword

This is a book for Dutch speakers entering the jungles of English. On their way they are bound to encounter the quicksand of prepositional phrases, the dangers of illogical spelling and the sheer frustration of verb tenses like the present continuous.

More than merely hoping to rescue the Dutch speaker from English's many grammatical traps, I especially want to point out the language's riches and joys. To understand English and speak it properly, you first need to know and appreciate the Anglo-Saxon culture – linguistic and otherwise – that underpins it.

English is more than a grammatical challenge. Often it is also a mind-set, an intelligence test and a cultural riddle.

Native English speakers have an advantage over the English speaker. They were born into the language and subconsciously indoctrinated into its unspoken rules and assumptions.

Not everyone can be born in Sydney, Cincinnati or Chelmsford. For those who weren't, and particularly for the Dutch speaker, *Native English for Nederlanders* is designed to be a grammatical handbook, a cultural guide and a handy reference for the elusive 'linguistic etiquette' that sets speakers of proper English apart from those who simply bumble along in the language.

It is not my intention to turn every Henk into a Hank, every Tjeerd into a Ted or Marijke into a Mary. Not only would this be an impossible task, it would also make the world a more boring place in which to live.

I can't turn you into a real native, nor do I want to. I do aim, however, to equip you with the background information and tips you will need to step into the skin of native English speakers and truly grasp the reasons why they speak the language the way they do.

Once you have done that, you will finally be ready to speak proper English with real aplomb – while ultimately remaining true to yourself.

I know that this can be done, as I took the same trip in the opposite direction – from native English speaker to a speaker of pretty proper Dutch – and lived to tell the tale.

Table of Contents

Introduction

Fifteen years into our marriage, my Dutch wife Jeanet turned to me one day and said 'I like you better in English.'

At first I thought we were facing a marital crisis. Later I learned that it was more serious than that. We were actually confronting a linguistic problem of huge proportions.

As an American of Dutch descent, I had arrived in the Netherlands at the age of 25 with a rudimentary grasp of Dutch, mostly of the *huis, tuin en keuken* variety. I could understand everything that was said around me, thanks to my immigrant parents having spoken Dutch to me and to each other during my childhood in the suburbs of Boston, Massachusetts. In most cases, I could even respond in basic Dutch, though I was unable to distinguish between *de* and *het*. I had managed to reach the ripe old age of 25 without realizing that it was *het boek*, not *de boek*, for instance.

If I didn't want to languish at my *steenkolen* level forever, it quickly became obvious that I needed to work hard and I did. I learned *'t kofschip*. I memorized which words took the article *de* and which took *het*. I figured out where and when to drop that most difficult of Dutch words – *er* – into sentences like *Er waren er vier*.

Then, having struggled to master Dutch, I was suddenly to find out, years later, that my wife actually preferred me to speak English. In my own language I talked faster, made more jokes, laughed more frequently, argued more furiously, but I also knew when to be oblique, when to be polite and when to hint at a subject rather than confronting it head-on.

In English, in short, I was myself. I had learned a new language, Dutch, but had remained true to my native linguistic culture. Speaking Dutch as a true American is like playing water polo according to the rules of basketball. It can be done, but not easily or at all convincingly.

Ultimately, I learned the hard way that the new language you learn as a non-native speaker cannot be divorced from the culture from which it springs, and that a proper command of the language involves more than simply stringing the right words together in the right order.

If I were going to learn to speak proper Dutch, I would have to become far more direct, like the Dutch themselves. I would have to drop a lot of the politeness which riddles English but which sounds so exaggerated in Dutch. In the end, I would also need to drop the superlatives that are demanded of English speakers ('great!', 'wonderful!', 'fantastic!') and adopt a more deadpan style. I needed, in a nutshell, to *doe maar gewoon* and pretty quickly, too.

Speaking good Dutch, or good English for that matter, requires that you understand and absorb the culture and adapt yourself accordingly while also – somehow – remaining true to yourself. It's a tall order but certainly feasible, provided that you are helped on your way by friends, family, colleagues and, I hope, a book like this one. Can you ever truly go native? Probably not. But even the status of 'near native' will bring you closer to reaching your goal of speaking good, proper, native English.

In any case, my own experience in learning proper Dutch later in life was the point of departure for a series of weekly columns I write in *Het Financieele Dagblad* aimed at Dutch business people who need and want to speak proper English at work. At first, I tackled mostly sticky points of grammar. But pretty soon I found myself knee-deep in murky cultural issues. I needed to explain, for example, why Anglo-Saxons are so formal and hierarchical and how this gets expressed in their language, English.

More and more, I started injecting personal experiences and opinions into the texts. For a financial journalist trained at Reuters and the *Financial Times* and now deputy editor of *Het Financieele Dagblad*, I was at first extremely uncomfortable about stepping out of the background of the story and into the foreground. But it was a necessary step. If I were going to explain how to speak proper English, I would need to explain how I learned proper Dutch.

The two storylines were linked. For me, learning Dutch was all about dropping deference, toning down politeness and learning up-front directness. For Dutch speakers in an increasingly English-speaking world, the challenge is the reverse – to come across as more polite and indirect, while at the same time mastering the subtleties of grammar.

Having come from the opposite direction to perfect my Dutch, I understand the challenge of speaking proper English. Partly it's a matter of hard work in the field of grammar and of rote learning when it comes to spelling. But above all it's a question of understanding the underlying linguistic culture. Once you've figured the Anglo-Saxons out, it's far easier to speak their language with ease and assurance.

Accordingly, grammar is dealt with entirely from the Dutch person's point of view. Dutch speakers make certain common mistakes in English because they're coming at the language from a perspective that is completely different from that of a French or Chinese speaker.

Wherever possible, I discuss the cultural differences between the Netherlands and Anglo-Saxon societies which account for these, often unwitting, faux pas.

Unlike most books about foreign languages, this book doesn't concentrate on the long, difficult words but on the short supposedly easy ones. As we shall see, it is these short words that you're liable to mix up, not the long ones. By the same token, I devote a whole chapter to the use of numbers in English, a subject that is essential to understanding and writing proper English but one that most books and teachers ignore.

One aspect of language that I disregard is your accent. If you are old enough to read this book or to be interested in its subject matter, then you are almost certainly too old to get rid of your Dutch accent. Given all the other challenges which English continually throws your way, your accent should be the least of your worries.

Your Dutch accent can actually be an asset. English-speaking people expect you to have an accent and enjoy listening to it. They consider it charming and 'olde worlde'. Besides, accents abound in Anglo-Saxon countries. Although you should do your best to pronounce 'th' correctly, be aware that the path to speaking native or near-native English has little to do with how you pronounce words. Instead, native speakers of English share a common cultural base which, unlike their accents, can be studied, adopted and even copied by the astute Dutch speaker.

In eight relatively short chapters, I hope to cram in all the experiences, attitudes and prejudices that go into making somebody a native English speaker. Usually, this process takes a minimum of 18 years but I am aiming to condense the highlights into just 160 pages.

At the same time, I attempt to illustrate why in my view the Dutch are so handicapped in speaking English properly. First, they have a utilitarian attitude to all languages, including their own. For this reason, they are unwilling to devote the time and energy needed to master the language. They mistakenly think: 'People seem to know what I mean when I speak English, so why should I worry?'

Second, the Dutch overestimate their skills at speaking English but underestimate the cultural component at the very core of the language. Because directness is valued above all other virtues in the Netherlands, Dutch speakers are insufficiently aware of what I call linguistic etiquette. In English, words, intonation and language itself can be considered rude. In Dutch, by contrast, you are considered rude not because of what you **say**, but because of what you **do**.

Third, by focusing on **what** they are trying to say rather than **how** they say it, Dutch speakers of English all too frequently fall into the trap of relying on literal translations from Dutch into English, many of which go disastrously wrong.

For reasons I will explain later, I have chosen to use American rather than British spellings. More importantly, even though the book is aimed exclusively at a Dutch audience, I have opted to write it in English. Good teachers of French or German or Dutch will immerse their students in the new language from the start, and why should a book not do the same?

The only difference is that I am not trying to teach English to beginners. My assumption is that readers already have a working knowledge of English and, indeed, use it regularly, whether it be at the office or on vacation. But I also know that, despite years of practice, most Dutch people never approach a near-native level of English.

You cannot learn English from a book, not even this one. But you can be made aware of the pitfalls and the rewards of trying to speak it well. My intention, then, is to provide a cultural, grammatical and personal guide to that most infuriating and fascinating of languages. If you are not a native by the end of the last chapter, then I trust you will at least have gained a better understanding of how to communicate effectively with those who are.

1. Language with an attitude

English would seem an unlikely candidate to be the world's pre-eminent language. For one thing, its spelling is illogical and inconsistent. At the same time, English grammar is complex and confusing and, what's worse, every rule seems to be accompanied by a long list of exceptions.

The English language is also far from being a unified whole, making its universal appeal even harder to understand. The two main strands, American English and British English, are in disagreement on everything from the spelling of basic words like color (colour) to the meaning of certain expressions. In American, a decision is 'up to you', while in British it's 'down to you'.

Yet for all its obvious defects, English has emerged victorious in the world battle of the languages. French, Spanish, Russian and German enjoy strong regional support but none of these languages has the potential to eclipse English on a world scale. Chinese, in terms of sheer numbers of speakers and the overwhelming potential of China's economy, may one day put up a good fight. But in the meantime, hundreds of millions of Chinese are busily learning English – and with good reason. English remains the passport to success for people worldwide, and this state of affairs is likely to continue into the foreseeable future.

Indeed, the day is not far off when more Chinese speakers will be fluent in English than the 385 million people who live in officially English-speaking countries like the United States, Canada, Australia and Great Britain. Already, 11-year-old boys in Shanghai play complicated, simultaneous computer games with children in Mexico City, Johannesburg and Vancouver, and the language they communicate in is English.

English, it would seem, is taking over the world. Like a virus spreading out of control, it is infecting languages and cultures at a dizzying rate. The Dutch need to learn English, in the end, because the Danes, Portuguese, Koreans and Brazilians are also doing so.

So many non-English speakers speak English today that the language is arguably no longer the exclusive property of the Americans, the British, the Canadians and the Australians. English belongs to everybody, not just the Anglo-Saxons, and perhaps it's about time that the world simplified the language and made it easier to learn and use, especially for all those poor Spaniards, Russians and Chinese trying to get to grips with its impossible grammar and arcane expressions.

A Frenchman, Jean-Paul Nerrière, has come to the aid of non-native speakers by inventing 'Globish', a simplified English that is stripped of its extremes and reduced to a vocabulary of just 1,500 words. His thinking developed during his years as a globe-trotting IBM executive. Countless times he watched Koreans and Greeks talk to each other in a kind of 'English Lite'. He began noticing that they understood each other perfectly well, even though native English speakers could make neither head nor tail of what was being said. (You won't be surprised to learn that expressions involving heads and tails have been eliminated from Globish because they're, well, too English.)

And it's not just the French who want to pare English down to workable size. In his book *Steenkolen Engels* Dutch linguist Marc van Oostendorp makes the case for letting standards slip. (Indeed, his subtitle is *Een pleidooi voor normvervaging*.) Why should Anglo-Saxons dictate that the rest of the world speak English their way when, after all, not everybody is an Oxford professor clad in tweeds and prone to spouting verses of Shakespeare?

This view, if I may be so bold, is a typically Dutch way of approaching language: language is a tool for communication, and must therefore be functional. Foreign languages are necessary to communicate and to cope in the wider world that lies beyond the Netherlands' borders. Anything that is difficult – like English spelling, pronunciation and grammar – gets in the way and can best be ignored. This, at any rate, is a very common Dutch approach. It is the linguistic equivalent of the *zesjesmentaliteit* that bedevils Dutch schools and puts the country at a competitive disadvantage to other cultures.

Still, such level-headed pragmatism has served the Netherlands well, producing a nation of savvy traders and successful business people. Today the same practical point of view should serve to convince the Dutch speaker of the importance of learning to speak English properly. The hundreds of millions of Chinese who are busily learning English are doing so with the intention of speaking as near-native English as they possibly can. For Dutch speakers to be content with mediocre rather than excellent English is short-sighted.

Proper English is the standard against which you will be judged, even by Americans who tell you that you speak such 'great' English. In my view, it is essential to understand where that standard comes from. As we shall see, English speakers and Dutch speakers could not be further apart when it comes to how they view their own languages.

Visual versus literary

The advantage of writing a short book about a complex subject like English is that it leaves plenty of room for sweeping generalizations. So here goes: the Dutch 'problem' with English is paradoxically also a great cultural strength. Dutch culture is visual in nature, while Anglo-Saxon culture is literary or word-based. This fundamental divergence in traditions has produced very different attitudes towards language.

To the Dutch, language is a **tool**. To Americans, the British and other Anglo-Saxons, language is a celebrated art form with subtle shades of meaning, much like a Dutch 17th-century painting or landscape. But it is also elastic and evolving and therefore contemporary. As a language, English is seductive because it lends itself to almost any situation, regardless of the speaker's own cultural background.

Before I am inundated with outraged letters from both sides, let me explain why I am painting this language picture so starkly. I am convinced that it explains:
- **why** the Dutch quickly achieve a basic competence in English but then fail to advance to a higher level;
- **why** the Dutch always prefer English-language texts to those in their own language;
- **why** the Dutch find it so difficult to give a good presentation in any language, and why they find it intimidating to be playful and inventive with English;
- **why** the Dutch underrate language skills in general and why they are prepared to accept second-rate English.

To me, the cultural split between design and language – between Dutch reverence for visuals and Anglo-Saxon belief in words – is clear.

In the past the Netherlands has given the world Rembrandt, Van Gogh and Vermeer. In more modern times the country has distinguished itself by its strong tradition of design and architecture. Where Dutch art was once highly detailed, it is now generally *strak*, a Dutch word with mostly positive connotations. The Dutch penchant for strong, unsubtle design in bold, primary colors is reflected in everything from the visual signposting at Schiphol Airport to the playful Dutch guilder notes (now sadly replaced by boring euros). Dutch industrial design is rightfully world famous.

Dutch literature, on the other hand, has been less exportable, due perhaps to the Netherlands' status as a small country sandwiched in between such literary giants as Great Britain, France and Germany. I am certain, however, that this is not the real reason. The Dutch are at their best when they are creating visual exteriors and interiors, not the internal worlds of poetry and fiction.

American, British and other Anglo-Saxon cultures celebrate their writers and their written languages far more than they do their painters and their visual heritage. The best example is Shakespeare, whose legacy to his own language is unsurpassed in world literature. Hampered by a difficult, illogical and frustrating language, English-speaking countries have turned this weakness into a strength, transforming their native tongue into an art form that has taken the world by storm.

 ## Vondel versus Shakespeare

I may be wrong but I can't think of any lines from Joost van Vondel that have been absorbed into everyday Dutch. Shakespeare, by contrast, continues to influence the language to this day. The Bard of Stratford, as the 16th-century playwright is also known, is credited with introducing 3,000 words and phrases into the language. We all quote from his plays and sonnets, often without knowing it. For Dutch speakers, the ability to drop a well-timed line from Shakespeare into conversation is an asset.

Common expressions that spring directly from his plays include 'a foregone conclusion' (*Othello*) and 'into thin air' (*The Tempest*). Some famous phrases used by other people are second-hand Shakespeare: Aldous Huxley took the title of his novel *Brave*

New World from a line by Miranda in *The Tempest*, while William Faulkner found the title *The Sound and the Fury* in *Macbeth*.

In business, a bit of Hamlet sometimes comes in handy: 'Neither a borrower nor a lender be; For loan oft loses both itself and friend, and borrowing dulls the edge of husbandry.' In another setting, try 'All that glisters is not gold' (*Het is niet alles goud wat er blinkt*) from *The Merchant of Venice* to warn against first impressions. (But remember that Shakespeare wrote 'glisters' not 'glitters'.)

Nearly every word game that you can think of – from Scrabble to crossword puzzles – finds its origin in either America or Britain. Other countries and cultures have translated these games into their own languages, but the drive to play with language – to see spelling as a competitive sport, for example – is peculiarly Anglo-Saxon.

To me, the best example of this obsession with language for language's sake is the long-running BBC Radio 4 program 'Just A Minute'. Celebrity guests are required to speak, off the cuff, for a full 60 seconds about a random topic without any hesitation, deviation or repetition. The game requires an amazing mastery of vocabulary, as no single word, including the most basic elements of the language such as the word 'I', may be used more than once. It also requires a remarkable gift of the gab to be able to speak on and on about a nonsensical subject. The winning contestant must possess a knack for presentation as well as a talent for bull-shitting. At its best, the program sums up the English speaker's love of words, of playing with language and of talking for the sake of talking.

Biblical expressions

Another instructive radio program from the BBC is 'Desert Island Discs'. For the past 65 years, this popular interview program asks entertainers, politicians and celebrities to identify which eight records, plus a book and a luxury item, they would take along if they found themselves marooned on a deserted isle.

For our purposes, the most interesting aspect of the program is that the castaways are assured that they will find the complete works of Shakespeare, plus the Bible, in their tropical paradise. This promise is designed to stop interviewees from routinely choosing either Shakespeare or the Bible as their one book.

The Bible is a rich source of expressions in English. Not everyone is aware that they're quoting loosely from verse when they say things like:

- 'Am I my brother's keeper?' (Cain speaking to God about Abel in Genesis)
- 'Eat, drink and be merry'
- 'I'll have his head on a platter' (Daughter of Herodias referring to John the Baptist (*Johannes de Doper*)
- 'Money is the root of all evil'
- 'The blind leading the blind'
- 'Practice what you preach'
- 'All things to all people'
- 'Suffer fools gladly'
- 'A leopard can't change its spots'

Welcoming and all-inclusive

The beauty of English is that it is a welcoming, inclusive language. You don't have to be an Englishman, Australian or American to feel passionate about it, or to feel that you own a tiny part of it. Unlike French or Dutch, where bureaucratic and meddling government-funded bodies watch over the language and make weighty pronouncements on subjects such as the *tussen-n* in *pannenkoek*, English recognizes no central, absolute authority. English is what we make of it.

In that sense, English is very much a language of our times. When the Dutch talk about an Anglo-Saxon way of doing business, they generally use this term as shorthand for an economic model in which market forces rule supreme. English as a language is the expression of these forces at work. The highest ruling body in English is not some government committee but English speakers themselves, plus the sales figures of the various competing dictionaries which they buy.

In English there is no official *Groene Boekje*. In fact, dictionaries often disagree with each other on the spelling and usage of words. The matter is ultimately settled by market forces. In American English, a word gains recognition only when it is included in best-selling dictionaries such as those published by Merriam-Webster. In British English, this role of arbiter is played by the august Oxford English Dictionary, but also by Collins. The more dictionaries sold, the more these individual publishing companies determine what is right and wrong linguistically.

And that is as it should be. English is a hungry monster beyond the control of governments, absorbing and devouring words at a frenzied rate. Experts who collect such data estimate that the language's vocabulary contains some million words – and the number is growing daily. This compares with the 300,000 to 400,000 words that relatively more static languages like Dutch, German and French tend to boast.

For this reason, students in English-speaking countries go to university equipped with not only a dictionary but also a copy of Roget's Thesaurus, a wonderfully English invention that is now also available online. The thesaurus traces its history to the mid-1800s when Peter Mark Roget first published a classification for words that goes far beyond the *synoniemenlijst* you find in Dutch. In his famous work, which has since been updated and recast countless times, words are grouped in such a way that users can see at a glance the subtle shades of nuance available to them when writing English.

Using the copy of Roget's Thesaurus that I took along with me to university in 1976, I find a wealth of wonderful expressions for words like embarrassing and awkward ('ticklish', 'mortifying' and 'galling'). Such notions do not translate well into Dutch because Dutch culture is more matter-of-fact and take-it-or-leave-it when it comes to social relationships. But just as the Eskimos have dozens of words to describe snow, English has a huge range of words to describe tricky social situations. As a language, English invites you – almost forces you – to build up a vocabulary shaded with subtle differences in meaning, and then to use these words and expressions carefully and creatively. This is its seductive character.

Love affair with English

That the Dutch have a 'love affair' with English is partly because their practical, opportunistic nature informs them that they are better served by English than by their own language in achieving their ends. All the more reason, then, for them to learn to speak properly, you might think.

Whenever and wherever possible, the Dutch like nothing better than to substitute an English word for a native one. An *uitverkoop* is merely an *uitverkoop* until it goes up-market and gets rechristened as a 'sale'. Any *winkel* with real ambition quickly becomes a 'shop' and so on. Dutch immigrants in America, Canada, New Zealand and Australia drop their language of birth with a zeal which is commendable but which also betrays a sad lack of attachment to the language of Vondel.

Closer to home, foreigners moving to the Netherlands have not, until fairly recently, been encouraged to learn Dutch, nor have they been helped by either government policy or society at large. I suspect that today's insistence on speaking Dutch has to do less with the natives' respect for the language and more with their fear and mistrust of outsiders.

Rather than embracing its own language, the Netherlands has been infatuated with English since at least World War II. Dutch people in shops and in government offices love speaking English and give new arrivals little chance to practice Dutch. I came to the Netherlands with a basic knowledge of the language so I was safe. But I see expats around me struggle all the time – not with the language itself but with the fact that nobody will speak it with them.

In shops you will encounter English-speakers mustering up their courage to order a *halfje wit* and then see the shop assistant switch into English at the sound of a foreign accent. The expat then soldiers on in hesitant Dutch, while the staff member continues to insist on speaking English. At a certain point, new arrivals, especially those expats who know that they will be living here for only a few years, give up on Dutch entirely and never learn the language at all. Expats in France, Germany or Spain, by contrast, will eventually learn the basics of the language because it is expected of them, because the general population does not speak much English AND because the natives themselves are proud of their mother tongue and want to share it with outsiders.

The readiness of the Dutch to switch into English is in part a desire to participate fully in the world at large. English is so attractive to the Dutch because it is international and contemporary, and the Dutch positively love to take on the world. Round any corner in the remotest part of Africa and you will find a Dutchman on his bike, communicating with the locals with a mixture of words, gestures and body language. The

Dutch are not afraid to speak English or any other language, and this highly positive trait should never be forgotten. It is one of the reasons why Dutch companies and Dutch managers play an important role in world business, one that is completely out of proportion to the country's modest size. It is also a very good reason to speak proper English.

Yet the Dutch, at their worst, have a deep-rooted sense of inferiority about their own language, or at least very little interest in it. This encourages an uncritical veneration of English, their passport to the world stage and to global challenges. At the same time, their utilitarian attitude towards language in general makes light of the hard work needed to speak the language well. English is more than a language. It is by turns a mind-set, an intelligence test, a riddle and, let's face it, a frustration.

Doe maar gewoon

The Dutch view of language is imbued with society's wider *doe maar gewoon* mentality. You are expected to get to the point quickly, without too many graces or rhetorical flourishes. Questions are not couched in layers of politeness, deference or formality, as they are in English. Information in Dutch is conveyed directly and with little fanfare. This is the linguistic equivalent of the *strakheid* that makes Dutch design and architecture so bold and compelling.

How differently English requires you to behave! The language is an invitation to heap on the adjectives, to be extravagant and even eloquent in your choice of words, to be witty and funny and clever. But it also demands a heightened awareness of social conventions, manners and linguistic etiquette.

American English in particular appears very casual, but underneath this relaxed exterior lies a sense of formality that is difficult to grasp for people brought up in a more egalitarian society like the Netherlands. English, whether it is the American or British variety, is a merciless test of one's education and schooling. Open your mouth to speak, and you're immediately pigeonholed, particularly in Britain.

For all its advantages and charm, then, English can also become a tool of snobbery. Because of its difficulty, it quickly separates those who can master grammar and ridiculous spelling from those who cannot.

In which other country would an election turn on a candidate's ability to spell? In America, for one. In 1992 George Bush Sr. went down in defeat to Bill Clinton in part because his candidate for vice-president, Dan Quayle, could not spell. During a photo opportunity at a primary school 'spelling bee', Quayle corrected a 12-year-old sixth grader who had written the word potato on the blackboard, telling him that he had forgotten the final 'e'. Quayle evidently thought it was spelled 'potatoe'. The incident, which seemed to confirm the nation's doubts about Quayle's intelligence, haunted the vice-president for the rest of his ill-starred re-election campaign.

Since English spelling is so difficult and illogical, the non-native might be forgiven for thinking that potato is spelled, well, potatoe. But there is more to the language than grammar and spelling. There is also the cultural component. English is a code as much as a language. When it's pouring rain and the elderly English gentleman at the bus stop turns to you and says 'Great weather!', you are supposed to know that he is being ironic and that you should reply in kind, 'Yes, isn't it grand?'

Similarly, if you are Dutch and an English speaker compliments you on your English, which will undoubtedly happen whether it is deserved or not, the typical response of the Dutch is to respond to the kind words in a straightforward way, earnestly explaining why the Dutch school system places such emphasis on English etc. But what is really required in this instance is a *deflection* of the compliment. Etiquette compels you to say that, no, you don't speak English well at all, that it's a miracle you ever got your diploma, that your accent is terrible, and so on.

Even native speakers must learn to adhere to the linguistic etiquette of their own cultures and to decipher the linguistic codes of other English-speaking countries. As we shall see in the next chapter, the Americans and the British find it a challenge to speak each other's language. How much more difficult, then, for the pragmatic Dutch!

2. American or British?

I am not a fan of the computer spell-check, especially when it comes to English. There are simply too many words that can trick the computer. But for our purposes here, the spell-check does come in handy. Click onto your spell-check directory and you'll find a long list of countries, each with its own variety of English and related spellings:

Australia
Belize
Canada
The Caribbean
The Philippines
Great Britain
Hong Kong
Ireland
India
Malaysia
New Zealand
Singapore
South Africa
Trinidad and Tobago
United States
Zimbabwe
South Africa

Do the same for the Dutch spell-check and how many do you come up with? Just two: Belgian Dutch and *standaard*, meaning the language as it is spoken and spelled in the Netherlands.

No one country exerts complete control over English, and this allows regional varieties to flourish and compete. Like a virus, English mutates wherever and whenever it can to ensure not only its survival in a world of many languages but also its virtual domination of the rest.

Of the many varieties of English, the British and American are the most important, certainly from a historical perspective but also in the present day and age. Which language should you, then, as a Dutch speaker learn to speak?

At school Dutch children traditionally learn British English. Not only is the spelling British, but the accent that the children are encouraged to adopt is British, not American. Outside school, Dutch popular culture is saturated with Americanisms. Except for the legions of BBC fans in the Netherlands, most Dutch people are fed a heavy diet of American English, in glaring contrast to the British English they are taught at school.

Worse, few Dutch children and only slightly more Dutch adults are aware of the very real differences between English as it is spoken in New York and English as it is spoken in London. Given this state of affairs, which variety of English should the Dutch learn, whether at school or on the job?

Many people would say that you should stay away from both and adopt International English instead: that is to say, English without the annoying local habits of the Americans and Brits and without any taint of colonialism. English was imposed on the world first by British colonialism in the Victorian age, and then reinforced by American cultural and economic 'imperialism' after World War II. For this reason, neither language is appropriate for a global age, or so many people would have you believe.

International English (also known as Common English, Global English or World English) is a worthy goal for any Dutch speaker, in the sense that your English skills should enable you to communicate effectively with other non-natives, like the

Finns and Brazilians and Chinese whom you will be meeting in your work and your travels. But I prefer another variety, known as Transatlantic English. This is basically a synthesis of American and British English that is familiar to and understood by both Yanks and Brits. The beauty of this 'language' is that it doesn't try to divorce language from culture. It does not live in some artificial cultural vacuum. Instead, it attempts to embrace the common experience of Americans and the British, the two nations which have had the most profound influence on the world's dominant language.

This is not to say that you shouldn't become familiar with other English 'languages'. Australian English is particularly colorful and earthy, reflecting the patriotic pride of a country once so isolated that its vocabulary – like much of its flora and fauna – is native only to 'down under'. Even the most casual television viewer will be familiar with such matey Australian terms as 'G'day' and 'good on ya' (meaning 'well done'). True to the stereotype there is plenty of beer-inspired terminology such as 'amber fluid' for beer itself and a 'liquid laugh', meaning to vomit.

But the language is richer than the Crocodile Dundee caricature to which we've all grown accustomed. The Aboriginal roots of kangaroo and boomerang are well known, but what about 'hard yakka', another way of saying 'hard work' that traces its origins back to the tongue of the native people in present-day Brisbane? Then there's 'furphy', a synonym for rumor or false report. This funny word, which you'll come across in the press rather than in day-to-day conversation, tells a moving story. In the trenches of Europe in World War I, information and rumors were passed along by means of the carts that brought water to Australian soldiers. These water carts were made by J. Furphy & Sons, accounting for the word still used 80 years later half a world away.

If you're going to Australia or planning to work with Australians, then it makes good sense to pick up the native lingo. In most cases, though, you will be better off concentrating on American or British English. But, given that everybody's time is limited, which of these two should the Dutch speaker choose? The short answer is American, and not only because I'm American myself. The truth is that American English influences Britain more than the other way around, and American culture – as expressed in everything from MTV to computers – is clearly dominant. If you speak American, the British will usually understand you. The reverse is not always true. For example, true British English might not be understood in those parts of the US where Jerry Springer is more popular than BBC series such as 'Cold Feet'.

In any case, the rest of this chapter will be devoted, first, to explaining the differences between American and British English and then to discovering what unites them. What sets American English apart is that it thrives on euphemisms and jargon, which can be confusing to people not from the US. However, the common denominator of these two strands of English is that they both set great store on notions of hierarchy, politeness and indirectness, all of which pose problems for Dutch speakers.

A Yank in Britain

When I moved to London at the age of 23, I thought I knew the British, and therefore British English, pretty well. I had just spent two years at Oxford, so what else would I possibly need to learn? London, here I come!

On day one of my new life in London I entered the local 'greengrocers' to do my weekly shopping. In those days, you were still served by a man wearing a brown canvas apron. 'Three zucchinis and two eggplants, please,' I said. This was greeted by a blank look. So I repeated my order, slightly louder this time.

Still getting no response and seeing other shoppers exchanging glances, I at last decided the locals in my neighborhood of Stoke-Newington must be confused by my American accent, so I switched to what I thought was a British accent and ordered 'eggPLAHNTS'. This didn't help either. In defeat I simply pointed to the zucchini and eggplant, paid my bill and left.

Eventually I figured out that zucchinis are called courgettes in British, while eggplants are aubergines. This won't have come as a surprise to Dutch speakers but it baffled me at first. Here was yet another difference between American and British English, to add to all the others.

Entire books have been written about the vast linguistic gulf separating these transatlantic partners. Winston Churchill said it best when he remarked that the Americans and the British were 'two great nations divided by a common language'. Most of the time Yanks and Brits understand each other, but that does not mean that they speak the same language. At best they speak dialects which the other is able to decipher.

The problem is not simply one of accent although, to be sure, this is the most noticeable difference between the two tongues to an outsider. The gap between an American and a British accent is caused by any number of factors. But probably the most fundamental difference is that British accents are 'clipped': that is to say, sounds are much more precise and kept under control, with lips, chin and mouth barely moving more than is necessary, whereas American accents are looser, accounting for the more typical drawl.

But for Dutch speakers, choosing between an American and British accent is the least of their problems. More important are the very real differences in pronunciation, spelling, idioms, expressions and vocabulary that crop up all the time on either side of the Atlantic Ocean. Even the formatting of dates and the use of numbers are quite separate, as we will see later in this book. In many ways, the struggle for supremacy in the English world is similar to the strife that once characterized Christianity. Who has ultimate religious authority: is it Rome and the Roman Catholic Church (i.e. New York), or is it Constantinople and the Eastern Orthodox Church (i.e. London)?

The British will often find Americanisms ridiculous and just plain 'wrong', whereas to Americans, British English comes across as stiff and formal. The truth is that many features of American English (the use of 'gotten' as a past participle of get, instead of 'got') are nothing other than vestiges of older forms of language that have since died out in the original mother country. Just as the French spoken in Quebec is 'older' than Parisian French, and just as Afrikaans carries with it traces of 17th-century Dutch, so bits of American English betray the fact that the present-day United States was once a collection of isolated colonies which remained immune from the changes that convulsed English back in Britain.

Be that as it may, differences between American and British English can be both funny and confusing to modern people, natives and foreigners alike. American school children who read British books laugh when they come across sentences such as 'Give me a fag, Richard.' In American English, a fag is a derogatory name for a homosexual while in British it is slang for a cigarette.

And then there is 'pants'. In American English there is nothing at all funny about this word. It's merely another way of saying 'trousers'. To the British, however, the word pants means underpants. The scope for giggles and guffaws, especially among children and teenagers, is nearly endless.

Differences in American and Britain English also plague the business sector, a world which most people assume has become universal and homogeneous. This is far from the truth, at least in linguistic terms. For example, there is a crucial difference between American and British English when it comes to the verb 'to table'. When Americans table a motion, they're actually shelving it. (In Dutch, you'd be putting it in the *ijskast*.) But when people in Britain table an issue, they're putting it on the agenda for immediate consideration. Get this wrong as an American in London, and your well-rehearsed meeting could end in disaster.

To understand the gulf between American and British English, it is easiest to think in terms of two categories: spelling on the one hand and words and expressions on the other. In both cases, however, there are no convenient or reliable rules for remembering which spelling and which words go with which 'language'.

Spelling

The u

One of the most noticeable differences between American and British English is the presence – or absence – of the letter 'u' in certain words. The British write colour, neighbour and rumour where Americans say color, neighbor and rumor. Other examples are:

American	British
favor	favour
flavor	flavour
favorite	favourite
harbor	harbour
honor	honour
mold	mould

With these examples in mind, you might think that the British always add a 'u' where the Americans have none. This would be far too simple and logical and make English an exceedingly easy language to learn. No, there are complications and exceptions.

Take the word pair 'honor/honour'. Given that British English uses a u in the second syllable, you would assume that the word honorary would be spelled 'honourary'. This is not the case: even British universities bestow honorary degrees, not honourary ones.

Then there's the word contour. Having seen the pattern of color/colour, rumor/rumour etc, you might think that the Americans would write this word as contor. No such luck. In both strains of English, it is spelled with a u.

Sometimes you have a choice when it comes to the u, at least in American English. Dictionaries of American English will allow you to choose between glamour and glamor and between saviour and savior. Both are correct in American, though the British acknowledge only the variant with u.

c versus s and z versus s

Very broadly speaking, Americans use c's and z's where the British employ an s. The c/s choice is mainly in nouns, while that between z and s arises mostly in verbs, especially those ending in either -ise or -ize.

There is a discernible pattern: in most cases, Americans spell verbs with -ize and Britons opt for -ise.

American	British
analyze	analyse
rationalize	rationalise
realize (realization)	realise (realisation)
organize (organization)	organise (organisation)

So far, so good, you might think. Unfortunately, things are not quite as simple as they appear. The verb advertise is spelled with an s in both American and British. And there are plenty of other verbs in both variants of English that end in -ise – such as compromise, surprise, supervise – even though you clearly hear a 'z' sound in all these words.

When in doubt, however, it is safe to bet that American spelling will almost always call for -ize, while British spelling will tend towards -ise.

Another fairly easy spelling question is -er versus -re at the end of nouns. Americans go for center, theater and specter, whereas their linguistic cousins in the British Isles choose to write centre, theatre and spectre.

Less straightforward, unfortunately, is the c/s option. On the fact of it, things look pretty clear. Americans write practice and licence. And the British go for practise and license.

But then complications arise, not on the American side but on the British. In British English a distinction is made between the verb and the noun forms of these words. If you license somebody to sell your software, the word takes an s because it is used as a verb. If you're finally allowed to drive, you receive a driver's licence, requiring a c because you've used it as a noun. But that's unique to British English. In American English both words are spelled with a c in every imaginable instance.

l versus double ll

Another salient difference in spelling is the letter 'l'. Although by no means a hard and fast rule (when is there ever a rule you can really bank on in English?), American spelling by and large tends to use a double ll where British usage requires only one. Americans write enroll, skillful and installment, in contrast to the British enrol, skilful and instalment.

And those are just the examples involving nouns and adverbs. Verbs ending in an -l get reverse treatment on either side of the Atlantic. In British English, words that end in -l preceded by a vowel usually double the letter when a suffix is added (cancelling, travelling), while in American English the letter is not doubled (canceling, traveling).

Words and expressions

Strange as it may seem, given the last few complicated examples, spelling differences in American and British English are not all that difficult in the end, if only because you can always consult a dictionary but also because these problems occur only when you need to write something down. In everyday conversations and day-to-day life, however, the potential for making other kinds of mistakes remains huge because Americans and Britons have maddeningly different words to describe the same thing.

We've already dealt with pants and fags. But these are just the tip of the iceberg. For example, if you're not feeling well in the US, you simply say that you're sick and everybody understands that you have a cold or a fever and leaves it at that. In Britain, to be sick means to be **physically** sick; that is to say, to throw up or vomit. The British say that they're 'ill' when they're sick in the American sense. Your average American knows what ill means but will hardly ever use the word.

Another good example is the word 'mad'. When you're mad in Britain, you're insane or barmy (a colloquial British term that is never used in American). When you're mad in America, you're angry or upset but you're not insane, at least not necessarily.

I could go on and on but this would produce a book on the differences between American and British English, not a book on English itself. But I will share some of the words that first threw me when I moved to Britain, in the hope of helping others avoid confusion.

American	British
candy	sweet
drugstore	chemist's
mailbox	letter box
the *mail* (delivered by the US *Postal* Service)	the *post* (delivered by the Royal *Mail*)
zip code	post code
sidewalk	pavement
bathtub	bath
French fries	chips
chips	crisps
fill out a form	fill in a form
take-out food	take-away food
studio apartment	bedsit
potted plant	pot plant (which in American would mean marijuana plant)

The clinching evidence of the chasm that still separates the Americans and the British has to be the car and the automobile industry. Now that the industry has gone global, it would be reasonable to assume that people would use the same terms and expressions on both sides of the Atlantic. Nothing could be further from the truth. Americans drive on divided highways, the British on dual carriageways. Americans pack their luggage in the trunk, while the British stow everything away in the boot. Americans watch the road through their windshield; the British do the same through their windscreen. Americans put gasoline in their car, the British use petrol, and so on and so forth.

It's little wonder, then, that each nation thinks that the other drives on the wrong side of the road.

Bank talk

It's not just the automotive industry which continues to use separate American and British vocabularies. Even banking, an international business if there ever was one, is divided along American and British lines.

American	British	Dutch
savings and loan associations	building societies	spaarbanken
mutual fund	unit trust	beleggingsfonds
checking account	current account	betaalrekening

When in doubt, use the American term outside Great Britain and its former colonies. The brute power of Wall Street and its institutions means that American banking lingo is more universally recognized than the British equivalent.

The great divide

So far we have dealt mainly with the nuts-and-bolts of language when trying to dismantle the differences between British and American English. More difficult – but also more interesting – is the cultural divide that separates the two languages. To speak proper American, you have to rev up your language, exaggerate and be brash in your search for new and more far-fetched superlatives. Why is this so? American English has, over the years, been subjected to repeated bouts of linguistic inflation, losing in the process distinctions like friend (*vriend*) and acquaintance (*kennis*) and making everything else 'wonderful' and 'terrific'.

To speak British, by contrast, you actually need to tone down your language. British English is introverted and understated where American is extroverted and over-the-top.

Of course, these descriptions of American and British English are stereotypes. But as always, they have a basis in truth. It is better to allow yourself to be led by stereotypes than to pitch your language incorrectly, which will surely happen if you are not sufficiently aware of the cultural components of English's two main strands.

My first lesson in these differences took place on my first day at university in Britain. There, in the historic dining hall of St. John's College at Oxford, with centuries of professors peering down on us from their portraits, American and British students gathered for the first time. In no time, the Americans were exchanging rather personal information with each other. It began with where they were from and why they were at Oxford, but soon spread to their parents' divorce and the death of their beloved dog when they were at the tender age of eight, etc.

The British students, meanwhile, were cautiously feeling each other out. No direct questions were posed, even fewer direct answers were received. Instead, the British were being their discreet selves, teasing out information and being circumspect in what they offered in return.

These differences are important for a Dutch speaker to understand. Compared with the blunt Dutch, Anglo-Saxons might all seem frustratingly indirect. In fact, within the Anglo-Saxon world, Americans are downright Dutch while the British are inscrutable.

Two examples will, I hope, illustrate my point.

'Interesting, interesting'

A fatal mistake in dealing with the British is to take what they say at face value. Many a Dutchman has gone wrong by assuming that they mean what they say. If you make a point at a meeting and the British chairman murmurs 'how interesting', you can be sure that your argument is anything but. Equally, your British boss means something completely different than you might think when he or she says 'do you think you'll have time to tackle that report today?' The message is clear although the language is not: get yourself in gear and finish that report – now!

Over-the-top versus underwhelmed

American culture values hard work and plenty of it. American students, eager to boast of the long hours that they put in, talk of pulling an 'all-nighter' before a crucial exam or the deadline for an essay. Later in their working life, this translates into long hours at the office and, more importantly from our point of view, endless explanations of just how busy our American happens to be.

The British prefer another approach. In Britain, despite the influence of the Thatcher years, it is still unseemly to be overtly ambitious and excessively energetic in the pursuit of goals. A true gentleman makes pretense of being merely an amateur who dabbles a bit at university or at work or in life generally. The true Brit of the old school does not wish to be seen as striving to get ahead. Instead, he tries to make it all seem quite natural and effortless. This is the exact opposite, in fact, of the approach that your average American will take.

As the above examples show, it pays to correct and adapt your language to suit situations that are either downright American or quite British. You need to be aware that Americans make liberal use of superlatives like 'fantastic', 'great', 'marvelous'. When translated into Dutch, these words will cause a Dutch speaker to think *doe maar gewoon*. But in American English, they are part and parcel of everyday conversation, thanks to a gradual process of linguistic inflation, and your own choice of words should reflect this reality.

Dutch speakers often resist rising to an American's level of enthusiasm when speaking English. This is because the Dutch tend to be plain-speaking, down-to-earth communicators by nature. They tell it the way it is, without too much fuss or bother.

Most of all, the Dutch have a particular dislike for that most English (actually, American) of greetings: 'Hi, how are you?' Note that this is not really a question at all, so there is only one possible reply, and that is: 'Fine, how are you?'

The Dutch balk at this exchange of pleasantries because they see it as superficial and fake. But their own language also contains a question – or a request, in fact – which is also not meant to be taken all that literally. This, at any rate, is how most Anglo-Saxons would view *Doe je de groeten aan Piet?*

Years ago, while on vacation on Vlieland, I watched a local dignitary entertain a crowd of tourists in the village's main street. He called an elderly British couple up onto the stage, subjected them to his broken English for about 10 minutes and bade them farewell by saying 'Do you the greetings to everyone in England?'

In English, there are several equivalents of *doe de groeten*. But my point is that this very Dutch type of pleasantry is far less common in an English-speaking setting than it is in the Netherlands as a whole. If you insist, the proper translation is 'give my regards to Pete', 'say hi to Pete for me' or, in exceptional cases, 'give Pete my love!'

Most of all, however, learn to say 'hi, how are you' without cringing. It will make life easier all around and put you in the league of the native speaker. If you don't, you will forever be stuck in Dutch direct mode.

The pitfall of Dutch direct mode is that, in Anglo-Saxon terms, you often come across as being uninterested, unfriendly or unimpressed, even when you're not. When asked to comment on a report or a plan, the Dutch manager might say in all honesty, 'Yes, it's okay' or – if he or she is feeling really positive – 'Thanks, that's fine.'

Unfortunately, although the Dutch manager meant to be positive, he has ended up sounding so 'underwhelmed' and so unenthusiastic, at least to an American, that the message is in fact negative. There's a wonderful English phrase for such situations: you damn somebody with faint praise. It is quite telling that there is no proper Dutch equivalent for this useful expression. So if you're going to succeed in speaking proper English, particularly American English, then you'll sometimes need to set aside your sober Dutch style (no more *doe maar gewoon*) and positively gush.

More concretely, this means that you sometimes just might need to learn to utter words like 'fantastic', 'great', 'wonderful' and 'excellent' with real conviction. If you force yourself to use these words in an English-speaking setting and they still feel funny to you, you'll be comforted to know that you've probably got it just about right.

3. Linguistic etiquette

While it is helpful to recognize the differences between American and British English, the Dutch should be even more alert to the characteristics common to all strains of English and how they differ from those of their own language. One of the most important (and the most difficult, coming from a Dutch perspective) is the need to be and to sound polite. Language cannot be divorced from etiquette. It is a cultural imperative.

English is a formal language, rooted in the keen sense of hierarchy of Anglo-Saxon societies. In the Netherlands, the Dutch spoken at school, in the home and at work is pretty much the same, broadly speaking. In English-speaking societies, certain words – especially swear words – are rampant in informal settings but exceedingly rare in formal ones.

A related characteristic is that English, unlike Dutch, does not 'tell it like it is'. English, as a language, luxuriates in indirectness. The real meaning of what the speaker is trying to say is cloaked in the words he or she chooses. Native English speakers understand the signals intended by certain 'code words'. The Dutch, raised in a culture of bluntness, often either miss the code words altogether or fail to respond to them correctly.

Pleases and thank yous

'Please' and 'thank you' are the basic ingredients in speaking English politely. Allow me to serve up two anecdotes that illustrate the difference between Anglo-Saxon and Dutch etiquette.

The scene: the number 73 bus traveling from north London to the Royal Albert Hall. The conductor (in the days that London's double-deckers still had conductors) moves down the aisle. In his lilting Jamaican accent, he says 'thank you' no fewer than five times in the course of one transaction:

Thank you (meaning, fares please!)
Thank you (as a reply to a request from a passenger for two single tickets to south London)
Thank you (on accepting a five-pound note)
Thank you (when returning the change)
Thank you (when handing over the tickets)

The scene: a bakery on the Overtoom in Amsterdam, mid-morning on Saturday. Exchange between customer and shop assistant:

Doe mij maar een halfje wit.
Gesneden?
Nee, maar ik wil wel een tasje.
Negentig cent ... heeft u het niet kleiner? ... Wie is er dan?

In other words, the entire transaction takes place without a single please or thank you being exchanged. This is perfectly fine in a Dutch context, but unthinkable in the Anglo-Saxon equivalent. The expression *doe mij maar* alone would be enough to upset an American or Briton because the literal translation is nothing less than an order: 'give me ...'

Thanks to our trip to the bakery, you can now understand why Anglo-Saxons in the Netherlands have to learn to drop their 'excessive' use of please or thank you in everyday conversations and transactions. It comes across as over-the-top and, well, *slijmerig*. In English, however, you can never say please and thank you enough.

Another word that is overused in English or underused in Dutch, depending on your point of view and your upbringing, is 'sorry'. This apologetic little word is used in instances that seem totally unnecessary or illogical. If somebody steps on an Englishman's toes, the victim will say 'sorry', as will the perpetrator of this mini-crime. Compare this with Saturday mornings at Albert Heijn, where shoppers bang into each other with their shopping carts without even slowing down, never mind expressing any regret.

This does not mean that the Dutch have no manners. On the contrary, they simply have different manners than those of their Anglo-Saxon counterparts, which trips them up when they come to speak English. In fact, seen through Dutch eyes, Anglo-Saxons can themselves seem downright rude. They do not say hello when entering an elevator, a shop or a doctor's waiting room, nor do they identify themselves by name when answering the telephone. They have no equivalent of *bon appétit* or *eet smakelijk*, preferring instead to tuck into their meals without much ado. They tend to ignore people's birthdays and it will never occur to them to congratulate your grandmother on your birthday, and so on.

Politeness, then, is a matter of culture and taste, reflected in language.

A liberal dose of the words 'please' and 'thank you' will help you along in English, but there is more, much more. True Anglo-Saxon politeness is linked to indirectness, another English trait, but also to a heightened sense of formality and deference. The more polite you wish to be, the longer your sentences inevitably become.

For example, you do not go up to a guest and say 'Do you want coffee?' even though the Dutch equivalent, *Wilt u koffie?* is perfectly fine in a Dutch context. The proper way to ask, in English, would be to say 'Would you like some coffee?' You might even say, 'Excuse me, but would you like some coffee?' Yes, these are slightly longer sentences and a bit more roundabout in their approach. And, no, you would not have to rise to this level of politeness when drinking coffee with a close friend or good colleague. But politeness in English is all about subtle differences and unspoken codes and about distinguishing between people whom you know well and those whom you don't.

There is a clear hierarchy in politeness. Imperatives ('give me the book') are considered rude. They can be softened a bit by the addition of 'please' but, depending on the situation and the degree of formality between the two people involved, a whole range of requests exists, varying from the merely polite to the very polite:
• Could you give me the book, please?
• Would you mind giving me the book, please?
• I'm so sorry but would you mind giving me the book?

Notice how the sentences get longer and the request itself becomes increasingly indirect. Translated into Dutch, these sentences sound absurd (*Het spijt me, maar zou u het vervelend vinden mij het boek te geven?*). In English, they simply sound polite.

So, despite all the differences we've seen between American English, British English and all the other 'flavors' of English available in this world, the overriding similarity that sets them apart from Dutch is this insistence on politeness. It is a way of thinking and speaking that must become ingrained if you are to learn proper English.

The problems produced by politeness – for the native Dutch speaker, at any rate – is that English speakers are easily offended, given their heightened sense of what is proper and what is not. The fact that the English speaker tends to be so indirect only compounds the problem for the Dutch. You may wind up offending your conversation partner, but you may never be told. There you are thinking that you speak wonderful English, while your colleague or acquaintance considers you an unspeakable oaf!

Inadvertent insults

More so than the Dutch, Anglo-Saxons can quickly take offense at words or remarks that are not meant to insult but still come across that way. Having a more heightened sense of politeness, they are more attuned to insults than you might think.

The issue of national identity, particularly in Great Britain, is a real minefield, particularly for the non-native. England is just one part of the country, and if you're from Scotland, Wales or Northern Ireland, you won't take kindly to being referred to as English. (Equally, somebody from Maastricht may not be amused to hear himself introduced as coming from Holland.) The more neutral 'British' is usually a safer bet, unless you run across a Scottish, Welsh or Irish nationalist.

For native English speakers the drilling in politeness starts early. Generations of school children are taught repeatedly to mind their p's and q's, which is another way of saying that they need to exhibit proper manners. 'Can I go to the bathroom?' always elicits this stock reply from teachers at school: 'Yes, you **can** go but **may** you?' Here the teacher is illustrating the crucial difference between the verb 'can' (the physical ability to do something) and 'may' (the permission needed to perform a task). 'Can I have some sugar?' is not incorrect in the grammatical sense but it is inappropriate in more formal social settings because it is not sufficiently polite.

Maple leaf

> Canadians are easy to offend: just call them Americans. Generations of Canadians have traveled around Europe with maple leaf patches sewn onto their backpacks, lest anyone mistake them for Americans. The error is simple to make because the difference in accent and dress is difficult to detect.
>
> Americans, being the dominant older brothers of North America, show no hurt feelings if you mistake them for Canadians. So when meeting somebody for the first time, you can either start out by asking 'Are you from Canada?' or choose instead to inquire 'Are you from North America?'

Once you have mastered politeness English-style, you will be well on your way to speaking English like a native.

As an English-speaker in the Netherlands, I had a reverse experience early on that gave me a useful insight into the Dutch psyche. Whenever I jumped into a taxi on my way to a press conference or an interview I would turn to the driver and say *Ik moet naar het World Trade Center*, meaning 'I need to go to the WTC.'

I meant this innocently enough but soon learned that *moeten* is a word to be avoided at all costs when dealing with the anti-authoritarian Dutch. The lesson was driven home by an Amsterdam cab driver who looked me up and down and said: *Moet? Moet? Meneer, ik moet helemaal niets.* Since then I've erased *moeten* from my vocabulary because I know that it rubs the Dutch the wrong way.

Similarly, English-speakers do not take well to curt or abrupt-sounding questions. As with orders and commands, most requests need to be softened by a cushion of politeness. In how many other languages would you expect to see a sign that says:

'Thank you for not smoking'? The message is crystal clear in its intent and its impact, yet the delivery oozes politeness. Or how about this sign that adorns the façade of the British School in Amsterdam: 'Please be aware that this is a paid parking zone.' The Dutch equivalent would be *Denk aan de parkeermeter*.

 ## Cousin Itt

Another sure-fire way to insult Anglo-Saxons is to think of them as a neuter, inanimate object. For them, it is inconceivable to refer to any person, dead or alive, good or bad, as 'it', unless it is indeed your aim to offend. (Fans of 'The Addams Family' will remember the character Cousin Itt, a three foot-high creature covered from head to toe in long tresses of brown hair. His name suggested that he was barely human.)

How differently Dutch and German, with their neuter nouns, deal with this issue. The final sentence in *Jantje heeft alle pepernoten opgegeten. Het is een stout jongetje* should be translated into English not as 'It is a naughty boy' but 'He is a naughty boy.'

In fact, there are only two expressions in which the neuter form is acceptable and even expected. Cards announcing a birth will say 'It's a boy!' or 'It's a girl!'

And Superman's arrival on the scene is always heralded by the words: Is it a bird? Is it a plane? No, it's Superman! But he, like Cousin Itt, was not entirely human.

The bottom line is that English-speakers are not at all neutral about the concept of neuter. Indeed, neuter in English means to castrate animals, especially dogs and cats. Keep this sensitivity in mind and you'll never make the mistake of referring to your boss or anyone else as 'it' again.

Expletives

Foreigners always marvel at how well Dutch children speak English. And rightly so. Unfortunately, one of the first English words these same linguistically-gifted children learn, and then repeat ad nauseum, is 'shit'.

The temptation is obvious: the word is short, sharp and extremely useful. When you accidentally whack your thumb with a hammer, there's no better way to express your displeasure. The same is true of 'fuck'. When things are really bad (when the shit hits the fan, as it were), what could be more satisfying than to shout 'fuck!'

Both shit and fuck have become universal for many reasons, one of them being that they are old and established words in English with a long and healthy tradition. Shit traces its origins back to Old Norse (skita) and to Old English (scitte). Fuck is, in etymological terms, a much younger word with a history of a mere 500 years.

The paradox of both words is that, on the one hand, they are used repeatedly in everyday life and heard all the time in popular culture, whether it be the US or the United Kingdom. On the other hand, they are frowned upon in polite company and cannot be used in any number of social settings, however tempting these words may be.

The problem for native Dutch speakers is figuring out when it is safe to use the f-word and the s-word. Things have become particularly confusing ever since Dutch television started to broadcast the antics of the famous British chef Gordon Ramsay, whose own television program on BBC's Channel 4 is, not surprisingly, called 'The F Word'.

The challenge for the Dutch is daunting because both the words shit and fuck have been embraced so enthusiastically in the Netherlands that their connotation as swear words has been all but lost.

In an interview with *Het Parool* during the 2006 election campaign, the VVD's leader Mark Rutte used the word 'shit' in answer to a question about his frequent appearance on popular television programs: *Ik kan wel een risicoloze campagne voeren, maar dan gaat het niet goed. Er zijn wel eens dingen waarvan ik denk:* **shit***, dat had ik liever niet naar buiten gebracht. Dat is het risico dat ik gecalculeerd neem.*

In the Netherlands, his use of 'shit' generated no interest or comment. To me, as an American, it popped off the newspaper page because, in an American or a British context, the word is ill-advised for a politician trying to woo the public. If George Bush or Tony Blair had said the same during their own campaigns, the word itself would have dominated the headlines for days.

It is not simply Dutch politicians who resort to the s-word and even the f-word without scruple. Contestants on Dutch quiz shows and cashiers at Albert Heijn think nothing of using this English swear word with great abandon. Indeed, a Dutch court once ruled that saying 'fuck you' to a policeman cannot be construed as an insult. In America, England or Australia, there would be no doubt that hurling these words at people in power (and in uniform, no less) is highly insulting.

So, despite the popularity of English-language expletives, non-native speakers of English should stay clear of the s-word unless they are completely familiar with all the people taking part in the conversation. Why? The correct use of shit is bound up with cultural codes that are impossible for outsiders to decipher. American teenagers will use the word at will among themselves, but usually not around their parents and certainly not their grandparents. It's a word that is forever being used outside the classroom, but never inside. It will be heard in the corridors of the courthouse, but never inside a court of law itself. The same is true – but even more so – for fuck.

Both words are a further demonstration that English is an exceedingly formal language by Dutch standards. There is a time and a place for using them, but in most settings, it is inconceivable to use these words at all. Rather than trying to learn when it's safe to utter 'shit' or 'fuck', it's probably best to banish them from your vocabulary altogether. At the same time, avoid their rather fuddy-duddy alternatives. Yes, you will hear some people say 'shoot' instead of shit, or 'fudge' instead of fuck, but these substitute swear words can easily make you seem old and un-hip well before your time.

 ## Pimp my language

True to form, Dutch speakers are taking to the latest 'bad' English word, pimp, with their usual gusto. Headline writers at Dutch papers love it for its hipness and brevity: *pimp mijn beschaving*; *pimp de premier*; *pimp uw stem*.

Pimp means *pooier* but is now commonly used, at least in youth culture, to describe anything that is cool and eye-catching, or any action that transforms something humdrum into bling-bling. The word's popularity took off after the MTV program 'Pimp my ride' (extreme make-overs of dilapidated cars) was first aired in 2004. For better or worse, it seems to have entered the mainstream, at least for now.

The problem with 'pimp' (and the reason that you shouldn't use it in polite society) is that its original connotations of prostitution and exploitation of women have not disappeared, despite the word's new respectability and popularity. It is not, in other words, to be used at a diplomatic reception or in any kind of formal business correspondence.

Deference, hierarchy and humor

The 1960s and 1970s wreaked greater havoc in the Netherlands than in the Anglo-Saxon world. Europe's Woodstock generation looked westward to America and imitated what they saw there. They donned the same jeans, took to marijuana in the same fashion and generally stormed the same barricades. A universal counterculture seemed to have been born.

Yet in the Netherlands these counterculture years ultimately exerted a far stronger and more lasting influence than they ever did in the US. America's hippies soon joined the workforce, settled down, took out mortgages and basically conformed, in their own way, to the rules set down before them by their parents.

Dutch society, by contrast, was changed forever. Gone were not only the strictures of the church but also the system of *verzuiling* that kept people in their pigeonholes. In its place came an egalitarian culture where distinctions of class, religion and social standing were frowned upon and virtually eliminated. Respect for one's superiors and obedience to authority were supplanted by a great leveling of society.

The phrase *moet kunnen* has come to symbolize the liberating free-for-all of Dutch society that so fascinates foreigners. The high point in this trend (or low point, perhaps, depending on your point of view) was the visit to the Netherlands by Pope John Paul II in 1985. In no other country has a papal visit sparked the degree of protest or the sheer irreverence (to wit, the birth of the term *Popie Jopie*, thanks to a satirical song popular in those days) that accompanied the pope's visit to the Netherlands.

In a sense, the papal visit brought home to the Dutch the realization that deference – the bestowal of courtesy based on one's rank or position – is not due anyone, not even a pontiff. But the death of deference was not limited to the Catholic Church. The erosion of authority quickly spread to the police, to politicians and to teachers.

It is hardly a coincidence that the Dutch language has, in recent years, spawned an action verb to describe being an adolescent: *puberen*. The Dutch expect their teenagers to be difficult and rebellious – indeed, if young people don't *puber*, this is considered odd and harmful to their psychological development, and the Dutch language therefore reflects this assumption by producing an unusual but telling verb. Anglo-Saxon societies still hold out the hope (perhaps in vain and maybe against all the evidence) that their young people will be well-mannered, that they will be generally compliant and that they will know their place in society's hierarchy.

This is a book about language, not sociology, so I won't belabor my point, other than to stress that speakers of modern-day Dutch do not have the same antennae for hierarchy as their counterparts in English-speaking countries. English may not make a distinction between *jij* and *u* but it does, paradoxically perhaps, contain more layers of etiquette, politeness and formality than Dutch.

As Dutch speakers often fail to understand this, they are easily tricked by the casualness of the language, especially as it is spoken by Americans.

The problem probably originated in the 1970s, when American bosses were sent to the Netherlands to run Dutch operations for big US-based multinationals. At the time, these men (for that is what they were) must have been a breath of fresh air to the local staff.

Here was a guy you could call by his first name from day one, who chitchatted with you about sports and the television programs he watched the night before, and who seemed downright approachable.

In fact, he couldn't have been more different from stuffy old *meneer Pietersen*, who was finally sent into retirement, taking his formality and his insistence on being called *U* (with a capital u) with him.

Appearances are deceiving, however. Beneath this cloak of American affability lies a keen sense of hierarchy. All too often, Dutch members of staff assume that the egalitarian tone of casual conversations with senior American managers reflects a Dutch-like aversion to authority and hierarchy. Nothing could be further from the truth. In truly American settings, bosses give orders and underlings carry them out. *Inspraak* and *meedenken* are as foreign to them as *hagelslag* and *haring*.

Casual language is fine in English, as long as the context is informal. A quick way of checking is to ask yourself whether you'd be using *jij* or *u* in Dutch. If you're a lawyer and about to meet the new senior partner from New York, you shake hands and say 'How do you do?' But when a colleague returns from a trip back home in the US, you can get away with 'How y'doin'?' More so than in Dutch, the social context in English determines how formal and how measured your own speech should be.

As we saw in Chapter 2, the linguistic problem is often compounded by an infuriating (from a Dutch perspective) habit of understatement and indirectness. This makes it risky to take words at face value. Beneath the politeness of statements such as 'would you mind...?' or 'do you think you'd have time for...?' lies an implied directive. Similarly, a murmured 'interesting, very interesting' from a British colleague can mean that, indeed, you've come up with a brilliant idea. Or it could mean that your brain has just produced a complete load of rubbish.

The only way to sail happily through these choppy linguistic waters is to develop other instruments than the spoken word. A well-calibrated antenna for nuance and body language is ultimately more useful than a grasp of the finer points of English grammar.

In societies that are far less direct but much more hierarchical than the Dutch, humor can be a handy form of indirect communication. Making a joke at times of great tension, whether in a meeting or elsewhere, is simply a ploy for defusing a potentially explosive situation. Equally, an overly polite or formal style of language can help to soften the blow of a direct confrontation.

For these reasons, for example, meetings in Anglo-Saxon countries are conducted using different language than in the Netherlands.

Dutch managers who regularly attend English-language meetings will soon find themselves picking up a whole new vocabulary. Consciously or unconsciously, they may also start adopting language that is far more indirect than they would normally use.

Why is this so? In the Netherlands, meetings tend to be outwardly democratic, giving people a chance to air their views and grievances. Meetings do not always result in any specific action or plan. Usually the goal is to create consensus. The accompanying language is therefore far more direct, even confrontational, although by the end of the meeting most people are on the same wave length and part company on good terms.

In the English-speaking world, meetings are more overtly hierarchical, and they are used to channel decisions that have already been taken down into the organization. Honest opinions and robust discussion are not always welcome, meaning that the real rough-and-tumble of a meeting takes place just below the surface.

To be effective in an Anglo-Saxon environment, it's sometimes best to coat any criticism you may have with a bit of sugar. A little flattery followed by a strategically timed 'but' can make a world of difference, as in 'I'm sure you're probably right but on the other hand have you considered....?' or 'I'm sorry but I think we should probably just discuss the point I was trying to make earlier ...'

In other words, you will often need to preface your Dutch directness with a bit of Anglo-Saxon waffle. But avoid the expression 'with all due respect'. Everybody knows that what tends to follow is anything but respectful!

4. English as code

As we have seen, language cannot be divorced from etiquette, at least not when it comes to English. In addition to all its grammatical idiosyncrasies, English is nothing if not a mystifying sometimes infuriating code. Meanings are often masked or obscured, and words are used to express the opposite of what they seem.

In a sense, English is made up of not just one code but many. There are any number of words or expressions that signal deeper layers of meaning to the listener. Get the code wrong, or ignore it entirely, and you'll find yourself floundering in English.

What are these codes or sub-languages? A couple have to do with euphemisms or political sensitivities, some with business jargon and sports, while still others are the result of the dominant influence of lawyers and court cases in Anglo-Saxon society. You may not want to absorb all these codes in your day-to-day vocabulary but you should certainly know that they exist and act (and speak) accordingly.

Multiculturalism

To a foreigner living in the Netherlands, it's hard to believe that anybody dares to use the word *allochtoon*. For starters it is an exceedingly ugly word, rivaled only by its direct opposite *autochtoon*. Worse, *allochtoon* is, more often than not, used incorrectly or imprecisely.

The word, which literally means 'somebody from another country', is used to describe every Achmed or Rachid in Amsterdam, even though they and probably even their parents were born in the Netherlands and are no more foreign than any other Jan, Hans or Klaas. Oddly, it is not used to describe somebody like me who was in fact born elsewhere. Clearly, then, *allochtoon* is a discriminatory word that makes foreigners out of fellow countrymen simply because their forefathers were born in North Africa or Turkey.

As a word, *allochtoon* is unthinkable in either the United States or Britain because it would be deemed highly insulting to citizens whose ancestors came from distant shores but who now hold US or British passports. The US in particular has had a long and sometimes torturous history of what the Dutch now call multiculturalism, and proper use of the English language requires that you do all you possibly can to avoid giving offense on ethnic or racial grounds. The millions of Italian-Americans, Arab-Americans and German-Americans would bristle at the very idea of being called *allochtoon* (i.e. non-native) and rightly so. The proper English equivalent is 'member of an ethnic minority'.

The rule of thumb in contemporary American English is that you call people what they call themselves. Take the term 'African-American'. This is the latest and therefore the most acceptable way of describing the millions of descendants of America's slaves. In the 1960s they were described as 'colored' or 'Negro'; in the 1970s the community embraced the word 'black' as a celebration of self-worth; and by the 1990s the term 'African-American' was invoked to put them on a par with all the country's other ethnic communities, from Irish-Americans to Albanian-Americans.

Given the above, it should be clear by now that you enter a minefield in English once you begin to describe somebody's origins. These matters are delicate and controversial, and the English language regularly undergoes revision when trends and attitudes change. It wasn't so long ago that Native Americans were called American Indians. As part of their struggle for civil rights and land settlements, Indians began to take offense at being forever linked with the country that 15th-century explorers were trying to reach – India – when they happened to stumble across the American continent. Indians are now generally referred to as Native Americans, just as the Eskimos now prefer to be called the Inuit in Canada or native Alaskans in the US.

Multiculturalism makes religious holidays particularly stressful for the Dutch speaker attempting to speak native English. You'd think that a simple 'Merry Christmas', followed by a heart-felt 'Happy New Year', would be an innocent enough wish to impart to colleagues and business contacts. But things are never quite that straightforward.

First of all, particularly in the US but also increasingly in the United Kingdom, there is cultural sensitivity to wishing people the very best on December 25 when they might in fact be Muslims, Buddhists or Hindus. But at the same time, a backlash is developing against the political correctness which dictates that Christmas trees in the city of Boston, Massachusetts, for instance, be called 'holiday trees'.

How can Dutch speakers avoid such sensitivities, real or imagined, in English? One option is to convey 'Season's greetings' or to wish people 'Happy holidays', thereby avoiding the word Christmas altogether. This will please some people but offend others, especially those who hate the fact that the religious meaning of the holiday is now all but lost. Saying 'Happy holidays' to people who belong to the 'Put Christ back in Christmas' movement is like waving a red flag at a bull.

For the same reason, be careful when using the abbreviation Xmas. To some committed Christians, it is insulting to see Christ removed from the word Christmas. In truth, though, Xmas is no slight at all. This abbreviation, pundits believe, has ancient historical roots. The X looks very much like the Greek letter 'chi', which just happens to be the first letter of 'Christos'.

If you're brave and decide to go for Christmas in its entirety, be aware that Americans say 'Merry Christmas' while the more restrained British traditionally say 'Happy Christmas'.

Sexist language

Just as English has evolved since the 1960s to take account of the rise of multicultural society, so has it changed to reflect the greater equality of the sexes. For some, of course, English has not moved radically enough to distance itself from a perceived paternalistic past. At the height of the feminist revolution of the 1970s, activists tried to get the word 'history' replaced by 'her-story' and 'women' by 'womyn'.

Although these radical proposals failed to win anything like general acceptance, English has certainly moved with the times, probably more so than Dutch. People now make a real effort to avoid constructions which assume that men are always the ones in a position of power. The statement 'The teacher should learn how to control his students' is perfectly correct grammatically, but it is now considered to be socially inept.

You can get around the problem by saying 'his or her' instead of 'his'. But this gets tedious after a while, just as it does in Dutch. A better approach is to recast the sentence entirely. In many cases, switching to the plural will do the trick: 'Teachers need to control unruly classrooms.'

In switching to the plural, you will be doing what many a foreigner has done when trying to learn Dutch. Rather than getting your *de* words mixed up with those that take *het*, non-Dutch speakers routinely take the plural route, knowing that this circumvents the problem, as all plural nouns take *de*. Another favorite trick is to switch to a diminutive (*boekje, boom-pje*), thereby guaranteeing that the correct article is *het*.

Sometimes you can avoid the third person or the plural altogether and rewrite the sentence in the second person: 'As a teacher you should know how to involve your students and keep them interested.'

You should definitely resist the lure of trendy alternatives such as s/he, (s)he or s[he]. They have yet to enter the mainstream and, besides, they are just plain annoying. As a non-native speaker, you are better off following linguistic trends in English rather than setting new ones.

So much for the gender bias in sentences. But what do you do about individual words that could cause people to think that you assume that only men are doctors, lawyers, et cetera?

English suffixes such as '-man' and '-ess' are slowly becoming extinct. Policemen have long since become police officers, firemen have been rebranded as fire fighters, and stewardesses are now called flight attendants. All other constructions involving -ess are equally suspect. Saying 'manageress' instead of 'manager' could appear to imply that you are belittling the woman who holds that particular job. Indeed, just as the diminutive in Dutch can be used to put somebody down (*vrouwtje, doktertje*), the addition of -ess in English can be regarded as insulting, with the obvious exception of a word like princess.

For this reason, waitress, as a word, appears to be on its way out. It wasn't so long ago that you'd be greeted in American restaurants with a bouncy 'Hi, I'm Debbie and I'll be your waitress tonight.' These days, Debbie will more than likely say 'I'll be serving you', extending a linguistic trend towards gender neutrality which, unbeknownst to her perhaps, has been going on for three decades or more.

Euphemisms

The Bible tells us that the poor will always be with us. But there are many terms in English to describe them, ranging from the have-nots to the broke, from the needy to the destitute, and from the poverty-stricken to the impoverished, not to mention low-income people or the working class. This 'wealth' of choice reflects not only the richness of the English language, but also the Anglo-Saxon tendency to dream up nicer sounding words for embarrassing or difficult concepts. A language that is as indirect as English will always fall prey to euphemisms.

The tendency to seek out euphemisms begins early and gets reinforced at every stage of an Anglo-Saxon's life. Dutch children (and grown-ups, too, of course) go to the toilet. In English they go to the 'bathroom'. This squeamishness about describing the place where bodily functions are attended to is a fact of life in English but an oddity for the plain-speaking Dutch. If you wish to speak proper English, you'll have to embrace euphemisms like a native. Most language courses, however, ignore them completely, making it all the more important that you be aware of these linguistic constructions and use them where appropriate.

Euphemisms stem from deep-seated taboos. Most cultures find death, illness and sex difficult to discuss, and nearly every language will therefore resort to euphemisms, which are nothing other than a roundabout, inoffensive way of saying something that might otherwise come across as blunt or offensive.

In English in particular, people rarely die. They 'pass on' or 'pass away' or 'pass over to the other side' – and these are just the euphemisms that involve the word pass. Before they die, they may well be obese (especially if they're American) but you would never know this from the language used to describe fat people. They are invariably 'big boned' or 'amply proportioned' or they simply have 'a full figure'.

If the dear and departed relative was also a criminal in his youth, he was a 'juvenile delinquent' who spent time in a 'correctional facility', never a jail. If he was ever unemployed, he was between jobs. And if suspended from duty, he was put on 'administrative leave'.

Although Dutch has its share of euphemisms, I would contend – without the benefit of statistics or scientific evidence – that English has more of them. The Dutch as a whole are less afraid than Anglo-Saxons to 'tell it like it is'. Plain speaking, Dutch-style, can sometimes be an asset in English, but only if you know when you can get away with it and which risks you are taking. Know your euphemisms and use them wisely and well. Remember that you are not so much speaking a second language as using an intricate code. Your message may sometimes have to be swaddled in woolly language that you would avoid like the plague if you were speaking Dutch.

In official documents in particular, policy makers bend over backwards to avoid calling people anything that could be interpreted as being insulting or discriminatory. The word 'blind', once a perfectly acceptable description of people who cannot see, has been supplanted by 'visually impaired', for example.

There are other reasons why words in English can fall out of favor. The word 'problem' is a case in point. In America it was first supplanted by the overly optimistic 'challenge'. When this became untenable (because people quickly saw this euphemism for what it was), business people and others switched to 'issue', a more neutral evasion. In American business, there are no longer problems, simply issues.

Why? It's a matter of managers wanting to sound upbeat and positive. Complaining or sounding negative is culturally unacceptable in American business. This poses a dilemma for Dutch speakers. Do you present yourself as the plain-talking, no-nonsense European? Or do you conform for the sake of ease and an amicable social life?

The choice is never easy. But whichever route you take, keep in mind the sensitivities that lie at the heart of politically correct lingo. In multicultural America, sensitivity to any real or perceived slight is huge. This, coupled with the tendency of Americans to take each other to court, makes people – and their language – cautious, sometimes overly so.

Legalese

The legal profession exerts great influence on the daily lives of Americans and therefore on the development of the English language. Don't take my word for it, just look at the statistics. For instance, there are more lawyers in the relatively small city of Washington, DC than in all of Japan. Whether in Washington or any small town in the US, lawyers crop up in almost every transaction or dispute, meaning that companies in particular live in dread of running afoul of any law or activist group. Or watch the ads on local TV stations in the US. All day long, lawyers are on the prowl for customers with real or imaginary grievances.

The fear of lawyers and of lawsuits is everywhere. Glance at the cv's of Americans applying for jobs and you'll notice that they leave out any mention of their age or marital status. Prospective employers do not want access to this information for fear that they may face charges of discriminating against older people or against mothers with small children. How different this is from standard practice in the Netherlands, where applicants not only tell you their own age but also give the names – and dates of birth! – of their children.

The language of job applications reflects the wider legalistic trend that is permeating Anglo-Saxon culture, particularly in the United States. Only in America do shouting matches between two eight-year-olds end in an angry 'I'll sue!'

Indeed, generations of Americans have been brought up on courtroom drama. In the 1960s American television audiences were enthralled by the series 'Perry Mason'. It is here that people learned such technical legal terms as 'objection' followed by the judge's 'sustained' or 'overruled'. Even today a good Hollywood blockbuster will have at least one action-packed car chase and one nerve-wracking courtroom scene.

Such courtroom drama is not normally available to the average Dutch child and therefore to the average Dutch speaker. This is because the legal system in the Netherlands does not infiltrate everyday life the way it does in the litigious US.

You don't need to be a lawyer to notice that American English is riddled with legal phrases, many of them designed to ward off any hint of liability on the part of the speaker. The result is often dull, weighty language, full of escape clauses and unnecessary jargon. When this happens, language is reduced to what is called 'legalese'.

Once you are alert to it, you'll spot legal phraseology everywhere. Even the innocent-looking term 'and/or' finds its origins in legal texts drafted to absolve the writer of any future blame.

Legal terms in English fall into two categories: Latin and non-Latin. More so than Dutch, English is peppered with Latin terms which originally sprang from legal texts and then entered the mainstream. *Prima facie* ('at first sight'), used to describe a legal case or type of evidence, has come to mean anything that is self-evident. Other Latin legal phrases that can and do crop up, though not in everyday speech, are *in camera* (in the sense of secret), *de jure* (in law/by right) and *sub judice* ('onder de rechter').

More troublesome, particularly for the uninitiated, are non-Latin terms. The language of contracts is responsible for the continued existence of formal words like 'aforementioned', 'forthwith' and 'pursuant to'. These are best avoided, otherwise you sound pompous.

Also be aware that common words can carry a completely different legal meaning. As in Dutch, a 'party' (*partij*) is not necessarily a social gathering; it can also refer to people involved in a dispute or contract. 'Consideration' is sometimes merely kindness but in a legal sense it is synonymous with *quid pro quo*: something ('consideration') received in return for something else. 'Counsel' is not just advice. It is another name for a lawyer or attorney. And should therefore never be spelled as 'council'.

Latin

In addition to legal terminology there is quite a lot more to say about the lasting effect of Latin on the English language as it is spoken today.

Latin has influenced most western languages, English and Dutch alike. You would think that this would be an advantage for Dutch speakers learning English. If both languages share a common root language, these Latin-based words should at least be similar in both languages, shouldn't they?

As always when it comes to English, things are not as simple as they seem. Yes, English borrowed heavily from Latin, but not just from classical Latin. This means that later, medieval forms of Latin were also absorbed into English, as was a form of Latin that was first filtered through Romance languages such as French, Spanish and of course Italian. The Latin legacy is therefore as much a hodgepodge as the English language itself.

This state of affairs can put Dutch speakers in an uncomfortable position, particularly if they attended a *gymnasium* and did their best at the time to master noun declensions in Latin. They will discover that English has borrowed 'incorrectly' from Latin, at least from the point of the view of a purist who learned classical Latin.

For the most part Dutch tends to follow the pattern of Latin that you'd expect if you studied the language at school. A whole host of words end in -um in the singular form and in -a in the plural. Familiar sequences in Dutch are *quotum/quota*, *visum/visa*, *criterium/criteria* and so on.

In many cases, English takes these same words from the Latin but then – confusingly – uses the plural form as the singular noun. Anglo-Saxons then add insult to injury by forming the plural of these same Latin words by simply adding an 's', as if they were any old English word.

This explains why you'll find yourself reading that 'the Netherlands has been granted a new herring *quota*', but also that 'the new members of the EU plan to protest against their individual fishing *quotas*.'

In many respects Dutch speakers will need to unlearn their Latin in order to learn English. They must be particularly suspicious of any word that ends in either -um or -a, as it may not have entered English in quite the same way as in Dutch.

For example, 'criterium' is never used in English. The preferred word is 'criterion', a borrowing from the Greek. The plural, however, is the same in both Dutch and English: criteria.

Another word to unlearn is 'per'. Dutch speakers will often be tempted in their own language to write *per 15 september*, even though *op* or *vanaf 15 september* would be equally correct and comprehensible. In English 'per' is used differently and not at all in the sense of time or dates. You'll come across it in formal English sentences such as 'please transfer the money as per my earlier instructions' ('as per' = in accordance with). In English, as in Dutch, the word is best erased from your vocabulary.

Meanings of some Latin words can also be very different. Take the word gymnasium. Although a perfectly good word in English, gymnasium does not mean what most Dutch speakers think it does. In England and America a gymnasium is nothing more glamorous than a school's *gymzaal*. If you're proud of having graduated from Amsterdam's Barlaeus Gymnasium, make clear that this is a high school, not a boxing club.

A final example is the word 'minima', a favorite among Dutch politicians. (As such, the word is more a case of polder-speak than Latin.) Like criterium, the word is never used in English and certainly not in the Dutch context. If you want to convey the same meaning you'll have to resort to 'underprivileged' or, if you're being really honest and wish to avoid the Anglo-Saxon habit of euphemisms, the poor.

Jargon

When English speakers are not peppering their speech with euphemisms they're usually resorting to jargon of the worst sort. Jargon is a sub-language spoken by insiders who share a profession or a love for certain activities.

In English, jargon – whether it be technical or political in origin – quickly finds its way into the linguistic mainstream. It is particularly prevalent in the business world, where no CEO worth his salt would dare give a speech without including such buzzwords of the day as 'synergy' and 'low-hanging fruit'. He or she will boast about 'thinking outside of the box', but will be loath to be 'out of the loop'.

The trick is to understand what the jargon means without parroting it yourself. Jargon is extremely susceptible to change, and if you're not aware of the latest linguistic fashion, you could find yourself spouting words that have gone out of style.

English business jargon in particular tells you a lot about the state of the economy and the relative strength of particular sectors. In the 1950s and 1960s, when advertising was coming of age thanks to the post-war boom, jargon from the advertising world gained general recognition. Fans of the television series 'Bewitched' will remember Darren's boss Larry, who worked in advertising in New York and who was forever coming up with new ideas and saying 'let's run it up the flagpole and see if anybody salutes.' These days, that expression is about as hip as calling something the 'cat's pyjamas', the English equivalent of saying *mieters!* in present-day Dutch.

The internet revolution and the computer industry generally are now the greatest motors behind business jargon. A favorite of mine is 'bandwidth', a technical term for measuring the amount of information or capacity that a computer or network can accommodate. It is now used to describe one's physical, mental or emotional capacity, as in 'I just don't have the bandwidth at the moment to put up with any more complaints from customers.'

Then there's 'off-line'. If you wish to discuss something with a colleague in private, but you find yourself in the middle of a business seminar, you might say 'let's talk about this off-line,' meaning when you're not 'online', i.e. within earshot of friends or enemies.

This kind of jargon can be entertaining but it's also highly contagious. Non-native speakers are particularly vulnerable to the jargon disease because they spend a lot of their time mimicking their native friends and colleagues. Before you know it, every Hans, Marijke and Willem will be talking about 'mission-critical deliverables', or valuable 'facetime' or even 'seamless solutions', just as their colleagues Bob, Mary and Bill do.

The truth is that such talk is ugly and pretentious. Yet if your boss and colleagues use these terms, and they're native English speakers, surely you should follow their lead and talk this way, too?

The answer is no. Try as you might to keep up with the jargon, your native English colleagues will always have a natural advantage. Rather than emulate their jargon-ridden language, you are better off sticking to relatively simple – and therefore highly effective – language. By avoiding the long-winded business jargon which English-speaking managers have inflicted on the rest of the world, you will come across as eloquent and sharp by comparison. Indeed, as the great Dutch philosopher Johan Cruijff once said, every disadvantage has its advantages.

How do you steer clear of the jargon that has taken up residence in the minds and vocabularies of native speakers? One reliable method is to live in dread of 'Bullshit Bingo'. This is the game that people began to play at shareholders' meetings and at company presentations in the 1990s. Armed with bingo cards full of rows of irritating buzzwords, they would take great delight in crossing off jargon as it came up in the CEO's speech. Five words in a row and they would then shout (if they dared) 'Bingo!'

With this nightmare in mind, you can more easily rid your speech of certain set phrases. When your superiors end their presentations with a slide on 'key takeaways', you'll know that, in plain English, they wish to impart 'important lessons'. If you think hard enough, you'll always be able to find straightforward language for tired old expressions ('meeting' instead of 'facetime' and 'easy decisions' instead of 'low-hanging fruit').

At the same time, avoid the American habit of turning nouns into verbs. As a manager, you should set priorities, not 'prioritize', and give people incentives, not 'incentivize'.

'At the end of the day' (another piece of annoying jargon to avoid) you don't want to be remembered for idiosyncratic language. Cruijff might get away with it, but you probably won't, at least not in English.

Sports as metaphor

All countries or cultures choose metaphors that work best for them. Although the Dutch may not be aware of it themselves, their day-to-day language is enriched by wonderful maritime expressions that can be traced back to the country's seafaring tradition, such as *tussen wal en schip*, *kijken waar het schip strandt*, *schoon schip maken* and so on.

In business, however, the Dutch metaphor of choice is that of courtship and marriage. Even the most intelligent CEOs will resort to toe-curling romantic metaphors at every possible turn when talking about an acquisition. A merger target will often be described as a blushing bride, the acquisition itself as a match made in heaven.

American, British and other English-language business people would not be caught dead professing their love for another company. But they will, whenever and wherever possible, drop sports metaphors into their speech and their speeches. Why? Anglo-Saxon culture, whether it be Australian or American, is sports-crazy, and the English language reflects that in a way that most non-natives never really grasp. This tendency to use sports idioms is further strengthened by the competitive nature of Anglo-Saxon society generally, where people have fewer qualms about striving to get ahead.

The challenge for the Dutch speaker – as was the case with legalese and business jargon – is to know a sports metaphor when you hear one, but to be careful when using one yourself. Unfortunately, there are very few universal sports, making it nearly impossible to assume that your conversation partner will know what you mean when you say 'offside' or 'sticky wicket'. If you are in Omaha, Nebraska in the American Midwest, then by all means drop some American football terminology into your speech or your presentation – they'll love it. If you're addressing an audience of Chinese, Italians and Norwegians in English, you will need to steer away from sports terms simply because the point you're trying to make will probably be lost on them.

This confusion arises because sports are simply impossible to export from one country to another. The United States may choose to call its baseball championships the World Series but the sport is hardly a global hit. Apart from Japan, Canada and parts of Latin America, there is very little interest in baseball outside the us. The same is true of American football (which Americans simply call football) and, to a lesser extent, basketball and ice hockey. Conversely, the World Cup in football (soccer to Americans) attracts only minor attention in the United States, despite the growing number of children, girls especially, who now play the game.

In fact, the only really universal sport in the end is Formula 1 racing, which might explain why an international Dutch-based financial institution such as ING is prepared to put up so much money to sponsor it.

To get a good grasp of English, then, it's a good idea to become familiar with sports you've never played. Sports like baseball in the us and cricket in Britain generate all sorts of expressions which, understandably enough, may make no sense to you at first and which are probably equally mystifying to the Greeks and Ghanaians you might be speaking English to.

These sport-based terms include:

- **Monday morning quarterback**: someone whose criticism is based purely on hindsight.
  In American football, the big games are played on Sunday, meaning that by the next morning every fan has an opinion on what the quarterback (the guy throwing the ball) should have done. A CEO frustrated by negative comments from equity analysts after the release of quarterly profit figures might mutter 'damned Monday morning quarterbacks!'
- In baseball a **pinch-hitter** is someone brought in to bat at a crucial moment in the game instead of the player originally scheduled. In business pinch-hitting occurs when an expert is brought in to lead a crisis-ridden project. It's nice to be the pinch-hitter but not the person bumped out of the usual line-up.
- A **ballpark figure** is a rough estimate, equivalent to *nattevingerwerk*, with the ballpark in question being the baseball diamond and beyond. When your boss asks for a ballpark figure, he or she is looking for an informed guess within reasonable bounds of reliability.
- If you're urged to **step up to the plate**, you're being asked, in metaphorical terms, to take the initiative, responsibility, action or all three. (In baseball, the batter stands at the plate.) There is also a cricket equivalent: **step up to the crease**.
- Anything that comes in threes is a **hat trick**, a term that originated in cricket but has since spread to ice hockey, where players score a hat trick by shooting the puck in the goal three times in the course of one game.
- Scoring a run in baseball has generated two expressions which, in American English, are now synonymous with great achievements: a **grand slam** or a **home run**. A grand slam is particularly impressive because you've managed to bring in all three men who were already on base, producing a total of four runs. Runners on base are called **ducks on the pond**, a term which means that you – the batter, in this case – enjoy a good starting position for potential success.

- In baseball, a **double-header** occurs when you play two games in succession. The term has come to mean a busy schedule, especially if the person in question is juggling two difficult appointments or jobs. If somebody refers to **late innings**, he or she means that a project is in its final stages. Baseball has nine innings (or periods), of which the seventh, eighth and ninth innings are considered to be late.
- Another American sport, basketball, is a rich source of expressions that are guaranteed to impress the natives but also to confuse the poor Hungarians with whom you regularly speak English. A **slam dunk** occurs when a player literally sails through the air and physically pushes the ball down into the basket with an air of arrogance and assurance. In more general terms, you might shout 'slam dunk!' if somebody comes up with a great idea. A **swish ball** is a ball that descends perfectly into the basket without hitting the backboard or the rim – a perfect shot, in other words. The opposite is an **air ball**: a ball that doesn't come close to reaching the basket or even the backboard. Baseball and cricket also have terms for failures that have entered the language mainstream: **strike out** in the case of baseball and **bowled out** in cricket.
- Cricket is all but incomprehensible to Americans, so few British sports terms have crossed the Atlantic apart from the more general exclamation **It just isn't cricket,** which refers to any state of affairs that is unfair or dishonorable in the eyes of right-thinking people. Yet cricket is a rich source of idioms in Britain and beyond. A **Chinaman**, for instance, is a deceptive feat of bowling from a left-armed spinner. And then there's a **googly**, a wonderful word that was around long before search engines called Google were invented. Like a Chinaman, a googly describes a surprising type of bowling achieved by a right-arm leg spin bowler. Basically, the spin of the ball changes in mid-trajectory, catching the batsman unawares. American baseball has rough equivalents in terms like **curve ball** and **knuckle ball,** which may be used in everyday speech whenever somebody manages to throw an opponent off-guard.

The list of sports idioms in English is almost endless, reflecting the habits of societies which love competition AND language. Dutch speakers should learn to spot baseball and cricket terminology and to use it when and where appropriate, despite the risk of confusion you may cause yourself or others. Sports metaphors are a way of playing with language and are therefore to be encouraged. Just as Johan Cruijff has forever enriched Dutch, sports personalities have performed similar services for the English language. Yogi Berra, the legendary American baseball player of the 1950s who went on to become a manager and coach in the 1960s and 1970s, rivals Cruijff for sheer linguistic dexterity. Among his immortal lines are:

- 'Baseball is ninety percent mental and the other half is physical.'
- 'In theory there is no difference between theory and practice. In practice there is.'
- 'We made too many wrong mistakes.'
- 'I wish I had an answer to that because I'm tired of answering that question.'

If you manage to score points in English like Berra, you'll be well on your way to speaking (and mangling) the language like a native.

5. 'Dutch' mistakes in English

Sometimes I think it would be easier for the Dutch to learn Chinese than English. As languages, Dutch and English are too similar. Both languages spring from a single source – the dialects of what is today northern Germany, which in turn have their roots in the deep fertile soil of the Indo-European language group.

This similarity between Dutch and English, and by extension also Frisian and German, is uncanny. Such everyday words as house and boat are all but interchangeable, underlining a familiarity that is sometimes a blessing but often a downright curse.

 Borrowings from the Dutch

English is rich in maritime terms that come straight from the Dutch (dock/*dok*; freight/*vracht*; buoy/*boei*). But the influence of Dutch extends far beyond the nautical. All of the following English words and expressions (and many more besides) have their origins in Dutch:
brandy/*brandewijn*
cookie/*koekje, koekie*
forlorn hope/*verloren hoop*
pickle/*pekel*
quacksalver/*kwakzalver*

The easy sense of familiarity causes problems for the Dutch. The single biggest one is that it makes them lazy and over-confident about their English. So many words and expressions seem and sound the same that Dutch speakers assume they can get away with learning English without doing any of the hard work – the memorization, the looking up of words in dictionaries, the constant practice – that they would certainly manage to muster for Chinese characters, grammar and pronunciation, or for almost any other language for that matter.

At the same time, the confidence of the Dutch in their ability to speak English can produce some terrible gaffes. In his book *I always get my sin* retired Heineken executive Maarten Rijkens has compiled a hilarious collection of bad English by the great and good of the Dutch business and political elite. In almost every instance, the mistakes he cites are made because people opt for literal word-for-word translations of Dutch expressions into English. Sometimes this works just fine. Just as often, however, a literal translation from Dutch into English winds up producing nonsense. In English, Columbus's egg (*het ei van Columbus*) has no meaning whatsoever, whereas the inventor's cry of Eureka! is common to both tongues.

To be sure, English is a notoriously difficult language, and every culture has its own sets of problems when it is confronted with English grammar and spelling. If I were writing this book for a French or Spanish audience, I would have to discuss the differences between *doing* homework and *making* a bed because their own languages have a single verb for make and do.

The Dutch have no trouble with the verbs do or make – but that's not the case with plenty of others. This chapter will be devoted to the three most intractable Dutch problems in English – spelling, small words versus big words, and verb tenses. And, as a cautionary tale, I'll close with three mind-boggling examples of how badly Dutch organizations and companies present themselves to potential English customers.

Problem #1: spelling

If I had a euro for every time I saw the word wonderful spelled as wonderfull in the Netherlands, I'd be rich. If I managed to temper my anger at this common mistake, I'd probably be a lot saner. This book has but one aim – to stop the Dutch from misspelling wonderful. And if it stops you, you will be getting your money's worth.

My pet theory for the prevalence of 'wonderfull' in the Netherlands is that the Dutch feel, deep down in their hearts, repressed by the rigidity of their own spelling rules. In the orderly, systematic world of Dutch spelling, there is one cardinal rule, and this is that you must never, ever end a word with a double consonant. 'Success' in English therefore has its Dutch equivalent in *succes*, while that most American of sports, basketball, becomes *basketbal*.

Of course, the real explanation may be simpler – it probably does make more sense to write 'wonderfull' rather than wonderful. If you feel full of wonder at some awe-inspiring sight, what could be more logical than to exclaim 'Look at that waterfall, isn't it wonderfull?'

Although hard and fast rules are rare in English spelling, here is certainly one worth noting: never end a word with the suffix 'full'. Trust me, there are no proper English words that end this way. Suspenseful, skillful, resentful, awful and truthful all avoid ending in double ll. Yes, there is the word 'overfull', a term used to describe an email box overflowing with spam and unanswered messages, but this is an instance of computer language rather than real human communication.

Lest the reader think that English, like Dutch, bans double consonants at the end of words, look at these examples: address, earmuff, jazz. What's more, there are even plenty of examples of double ll's at the end of words, at least in American English:

distill, instill, fulfill. Yet for some reason, a combination of double ll's as in the fictitious wonderfull simply does not exist.

Do not waste your time trying to figure out why wonderful has one 'l' but distill two. There is neither rhyme nor reason to most English spellings. When you come right down to it, there are barely any rules to speak of. In English, you can't memorize spelling rules; it's the individual spellings of words that you have to learn by heart.

The most famous rule – one which every schoolboy and girl can recite from America to Australia – is 'i before e except after c'. Say it to yourself out loud ('eye before ee except after cee') and you'll find that it rhymes.

This rule is designed to help native English speakers cope with such words as receipt and receive. Having learned to spell words like lie, shield, and pier, Americans and other English speakers would be sorely tempted to write 'recieve' and 'reciept' if they hadn't memorized this rhyme at school as 10-year-olds.

But the problem with spelling rules in English (and all grammatical rules, if the truth be known) is that the list of exceptions is often longer than the original rule. Once you've learned 'i before e except after c', you then have to remember that there is a whole host of ei-constructions that follow all sorts of letters besides c. Think of 'neighbor' and 'weigh', for instance, and what about 'protein' and 'seismology'?

History of spelling

By now, the typical Dutch reader may feel irritation at the sheer stupidity of English, at the lack of the *Gründlichkeit* that makes German, and by extension Dutch, so satisfying to those who hate surprises. If all three languages have a common ancestor in northern German dialects, then why has English deviated quite so much from the standards of logic that make learning other Germanic languages relatively easy?

The history of English is a tale of successive invasions by other languages, reflecting the turbulent history of England itself. To summarize the convolutions of English in a few hundred words does not do justice to the changes to which the language has been subjected over the past 2000 years, but it does help to explain why English is such a mishmash of rules and grammatical systems – and ultimately why spelling English is such a challenge.

The British Isles were first inhabited by Celtic tribes, each with its own local and regional variations of the vernacular. Starting in the year 449, the British Isles were overrun by tribes like the Angles, Saxons, Frisians and Jutes from the present-day northern Netherlands and northwestern Germany, producing the term 'Anglo-Saxon' that we still use today and sowing the seeds of English as it has come to be spoken.

The next cataclysmic event, both historically and linguistically, was the Norman Conquest of 1066. This put a French-speaking elite from Normandy in ascendancy for more than three hundred years, ushering in a period when French held sway at the royal court and in the law courts and English was pushed to the margins of society. English reasserted itself around 1400. By now it had become a versatile language which had absorbed Celtic, Nordic, Latin, Greek and French elements but remained true to many of the Germanic tenets of the original Anglo-Saxon invaders.

This 1000-year sweep of history can be conveniently broken down into three periods, each of which is associated with a major literary work or author. Old English, the language as it had developed from 449 to 1066, is the most closely associated with the epic poem *Beowulf*. The poem is unreadable by modern English-speakers without a rigorous training in Old English.

The Norman period saw the rise of Middle English, the language in which Chaucer wrote his famous *Canterbury Tales*. It wasn't until Shakespeare in the late 1500s that modern English emerged as we know it today. By then, English had become all but unrecognizable from its original roots. It was a language full of silent letters (the final 'e' in most words, for example, and the unpronounced initial 'k' and 'g' in words like know and gnaw) and idiosyncratic spellings.

The most interesting point for our purposes is that English was once organized in ways that would make Dutch speakers feel very much at home. In fact, if you look closely enough at Old English, you see the ghosts of ancient forms of Dutch and German struggling to emerge.

For instance, the language had three genders: masculine, feminine and neuter. The Old English word for sun, sunna, was feminine, while moon, mona, was masculine, mirroring the set-up in modern-day German. The language also had five cases. Nouns, pronouns and adjectives were all inflected to match the required case.

Believe it or not, English words were also once pronounced the way they were spelled. In the Old English word for knight, cniht, the c was fully pronounced. It was only hundreds of years later that the 'k' and 'gh' in present-day knight would fall silent, producing a word whose pronunciation bears little relation to its spelling.

Today, English is still riddled with words that would sound almost like Dutch if you restored the guttural 'g' and 'gh' sounds that the original Anglo-Saxons uttered. Pronounce 'enough' in a Dutch way and you get something like 'enug'. From there, it is only a small step to *genoeg* in Dutch and *genug* in German. The same holds true for night (*nacht*), eight (*acht*) and so on.

Quite a few plural nouns in English end in -en, just as German and Dutch nouns do. In fact, up until Shakespeare's day it was just as common to form plurals by tacking on -en as it was to add -s. This old principle is reflected in modern-day words such as oxen, women and children. Another vestige of Germanic influence is still clearly visible in modern English verbs that end in -en: sharpen, dampen, enliven. The same is true for constructions involving be- at the beginning of verbs: bequeath, bestow, betroth.

If older forms of German, Dutch and English were once so obviously linked and almost interchangeable, how do we account for the current state of affairs, particularly the highly illogical pattern of spelling? Some six hundred years ago – say, just after Chaucer but well before Shakespeare – English underwent what is called the 'great vowel shift'. For reasons that are not entirely clear, the forebears of today's Britons began pronouncing their vowels differently. Eventually, the pronunciation of English – including consonants – changed dramatically but its spelling remained relatively untouched, producing a divergence between the two that has hampered the learning of English ever since.

At the same time, English continued to be spoken and spelled differently in various parts of present-day England. Over time, the London dialect won out over all others in terms of the spoken language, but spelling remained and remains highly erratic.

Today, there are 46 speech sounds (21 vowel sounds and 25 consonants) in English, more than in most European languages, but some 1,100 different ways of spelling them. Linguists estimate that the spelling of 15 percent of words in the English dictionary follows no discernible pattern of any kind. A further 50 percent deviates from the dominant pattern. This explains why the sh-sound can be produced in a straightforward fashion in a word like 'should' but also in surprising ways as in 'delicious'.

The ultimate solution to learning English spelling, therefore, is to buy a dictionary and use it. The energy spent feeling irritated by the language can best be channelled into the effort needed to tackle the other common spelling mistakes Dutch people make.

Lower and upper case

For a language so closely linked to German, Dutch has a surprising tendency to favor lower-case letters. Whereas German capitalizes the first letter of just about every noun, Dutch is a language of small letters.

I'll resist the temptation to concoct a theory linking the country's size with its predilection for small letters. But you as a Dutch speaker must resist the temptation to substitute lower-case letters for upper-case ones when it comes to spelling English properly. If not, your chances of writing English like a native will be pretty slim.

In English, whole categories of words are spelled with a capital letter in instances where Dutch speakers would use a lower-case equivalent. All months of the year and all days of the week take a capital. Each word in an address must also begin with a capital. Fifth Avenue in New York and Bond Street in London may never be written in any other way.

The same holds true for abbreviations, particularly in company names. Dutch readers of the financial press will be used to seeing bv or nv So-and-So, but the English equivalents of these abbreviations – Corp., Inc., Ltd., Plc. – must always begin with a capital letter.

Remember too that the first letter of titles and honorifics (Prof., Dr., Mr. and Mrs.) is exclusively upper-case in English, a reversal of the situation in Dutch. While you're at it, learn not to use *mr.* if you mean to say that somebody has a legal degree. There is no equivalent to *meester* in English. To use the abbreviation *mr.* is to invite people to think that you've made a mistake and meant *Mr.* (*de heer*) instead. It goes without saying that this problem is compounded if the lawyer in question is a woman.

Proper use of the apostrophe

The Dutch, for understandable reasons, are prone to using apostrophes to create plural nouns. After all, that's what you do in Dutch whenever a word would otherwise be pronounced incorrectly (*baby's* and so on). In English, a word ending in -y in the singular drops the -y in the plural and adds -ies. Many Dutch speakers know this intuitively but they still insist on including an apostrophe, creating such abominations as babie's.

Barring some very exceptional cases that need not concern us too much here (the spelling of lower-case plural letters and abbreviations like p's and q's and cv's, for instance), apostrophes are never used to form plurals in English, at least not in proper English. Yes, native speakers make this mistake all the time, too, but this is no reason for non-natives to follow suit.

Instead, simply stick to adding -s or -es in most cases to signify a plural noun. And remember that the -es (like the apostrophe in Dutch) is needed wherever and whenever a plural would be near-impossible to pronounce (potatoes, mosquitoes etc).

't kofschip in English

When I moved to Amsterdam from London in 1983, I had to get used to all sorts of new things, despite my Dutch background. Among the novelties was the food. People around me ate *filet Americain*, a form of raw meat that most Americans, me included, have not heard of and would never eat. Another mysterious culinary term was something called cornet beef. In English, a cornet is another name for a trumpet, but what could the connection between meat and a musical instrument possibly be?

The mystery eventually cleared itself up. When the Dutch say 'cornet beef', they actually mean corned beef, the cooked meat preserved in brine which is most closely associated with the Irish, with St. Patrick's Day celebrations in the United States and with war-time rationing.

This was my first 'taste' of the Dutch habit of pronouncing the letter d at the end of a word as a t. Where Anglo-Saxons say and hear corned beef, the Dutch say and hear something akin to *kornet-bief.*

The problem of t's and d's is, of course, familiar to anyone – the Dutch included – who has tried to learn *Nederlands* and become acquainted with *'t kofschip*. Of all Dutch spelling rules, this is the trickiest to master. The reason is as obvious as corned beef is salty: the Dutch are blessed with a language that is pronounced the way it is spelled except, unfortunately, when it comes to certain letters, notably t's, d's, v's and f's.

These letters cause huge spelling problems in Dutch. The d in *geschaad* sounds just like the t in *gemaakt*. And when Dutch speakers switch to English, they take their spelling mistakes with them.

The problem of d's and t's is easy to explain in terms of linguistics and the physical exertion that is needed to make our mouths form sounds. Consonants tend to come in pairs. On the one hand, you have voiced consonants like b, d, v and z, with the 'voiced' part meaning that you need to vibrate your vocal cords to produce the right sound. Each of these voiced consonants has its unvoiced equivalent: p, t, f and s.

In Dutch (but not in English!) the voiced consonant 'd' is 'devoiced' when it occurs at the end of a word. Essentially, the d becomes a t. So, in Dutch, bed sounds the same as the English word 'bet'.

If you live in the Netherlands, you become a connoisseur of the problems the Dutch have with d/t in English. When the 'Batman' movie first came out, I had a field day noting down all the instances in the Dutch press when the film reviewer slipped up and started writing 'Badman'. Elsewhere, you see people write 'feetback' when they mean 'feedback', or 'electricity grit' when they mean to say 'grid'. Even that most famous of export products, *nederwiet*, betrays the inability of the Dutch language to distinguish properly between the sounds 'd' and 't' when they come at the end of words. The source of this word is, of course, the English word 'weed', 1970s slang for marijuana.

Another example is the mixing up of the spelling of send and sent, caused by the Dutch habit of pronouncing these two English words in almost the exact same way. In the following sentence they are used correctly: 'I will sen*d* you the package again tomorrow if I hear that it was not sen*t*, as promised, yesterday.' Dutch speakers have an almost irresistible urge to use 'd' rather than 't', even when using the past participle (*voltooid deelwoord*).

To speak and write English like a native, you must master consonant pairs. Frenchmen or Spaniards will not make the same spelling mistakes because they are not burdened by '*t kofschip* to begin with. (Don't worry, though, other Europeans make plenty of other spelling mistakes in English, too.)

Once you've mastered the d and the t, it is time to move on to other offenders, chiefly the v and the f. The Dutch are forever spelling 'live' and 'life' incorrectly because their own language background prevents them from hearing the difference in sound. A native English speaker will not foul up 'live' and 'life' for the good reason that he knows – and hears – that they sound completely different. The first word contains a vibrated (voiced) consonant – the v – but the second does not.

How can you best avoid such confusion? Remember that 'life' is a noun and can only be used as such. 'Live', by contrast, can be used as a verb, adjective or adverb. The sentence 'Live your life as though every day were your last' illustrates the proper use of live as a verb and life as a noun.

The confusion among Dutch speakers usually arises in situations in which they want to describe a radio or television broadcast that is transmitted as events unfold. In English, such broadcasts are deemed to be 'live', not 'life'.

The third troublesome consonant pair for Dutch speakers is 'p' and 'b'. Again, because of pronunciation problems stemming from Dutch, people are heard to say 'spare rip' instead of 'spare rib' and 'crap salad' instead of 'crab salad'. (Crap, of course, is slang for *stront*.)

Although all Dutch speakers struggle with these consonant pairs, both in spelling and in pronunciation, those who hail from Amsterdam face an uphill battle. People who speak Dutch with a pronounced Amsterdam accent tend not to pronounce z's and v's in their own language (*De son in de see sien sakken*), never mind in English, putting them at a distinct handicap when it comes to perfecting their language skills.

But whether you come from Amsterdam or Zutphen, the bad news is that you can't leave *'t kofschip* behind when you move from Dutch into English. The good news, though, is that an awareness of the spelling problems involving d-t, v-f and b-p will not only help you to write words in English properly but also train you to pronounce them like a native.

Problem #2: small words and big words

When learning languages we tend to allow ourselves to get intimidated by the big words we come across. In English, words like 'thoroughly', 'penultimate', 'resuscitation' and 'invigorating' – to give just a few examples after dipping randomly into the dictionary – can be real tongue-twisters for non-native speakers, and they will take up far too much of your time if you let them.

As it happens, small words are actually a bigger impediment to learning a language like English properly than the complicated long words. For one thing, of course, small words are far more common. They're everywhere, in fact, whereas big words are the exception rather than the rule, certainly when it comes to everyday speech but also in most texts.

You know you're finally becoming adept at a language when you have complete mastery over the little words. In French, a sentence with a succession of deceptively tricky words like *y* and *en* (*il y'en a quatre*) is quite difficult to pull off. I remember feeling pleased when I could throw out the line *er zijn er vier* in Dutch, because the sentence contained not one but two instances of that fiendishly difficult word *er*. In the English equivalent of this sentence ('There are four of them'), the Dutch *er* gets translated in two different ways and requires a total of three words to convey the same sense of the double *er*.

Small words: if

So what's the worst offender in English when it comes to small words? For Dutch speakers, it is undoubtedly the word 'if'. And again, the culprit is not so much English as Dutch itself, which people naturally enough use as a reference when they switch languages.

'If' is not a difficult word to spell. It is, however, a difficult word to use if you're used to Dutch, where the word *als* has, over the years, come to take on two meanings: 'if' and 'when'. The problem this creates in English is serious, as it leads to mistakes that no native speaker would ever make. All too often, a business letter or email will end with the sentence 'Please let me know when you're interested in receiving more information.' Or 'When you're home tomorrow, please give me a call.'

In both sentences the Dutch speaker has interchanged 'if' and 'when'. In English, unlike in Dutch, these words have very separate meanings. (It's true that Dutch also has two separate words for such instances, *indien* and *wanneer*, but they are hardly ever used in the English sense of the words, and certainly not in informal speech.)

The key to choosing between 'if' and 'when' is knowing the probability of something happening. If it is possible that an event may not occur, use 'if'. If you're quite sure that a particular situation will arise, use 'when'.

With these basic rules in mind, it should now be obvious why the sentence 'please send me an email when interested' can come across as arrogant. It is, in English at any rate, presumptuous to assume that your proposal will eventually be accepted. By resorting to 'if', you acknowledge that this is an offer that can be refused.

The difference between 'if' and 'when' is all-important. Consider these two examples: 'If I take a day off, I constantly think about work', and 'When I take a day off, I can always be reached at home.' The first construction implies that a day off is rare, while the second suggests that it's pretty common.

A mental calculation of probability is therefore essential before deciding whether to use 'if' or 'when'. The phrase 'if I die' is, in most instances, nonsensical because death is a certainty for us all. For this reason, 'when I die' would seem to be the only possible construction in English.

This is not the case, however. Generations of American and British children learn a key linguistic lesson when reciting their bedtime prayers:

> Now I lay me down to sleep,
> I pray the Lord my soul to keep;
> If I die before I wake,
> I pray the Lord my soul to take.
> *New England Primer (1737)*

The addition of 'before I wake' lengthens the odds considerably that the child won't make it through the night, explaining why the use of 'if' is eminently sensible. In the long run, of course, and in most circumstances, the most common phrase would still be 'when I die'.

With prayers like these, it's a miracle that the English manage to get any sleep at all. But it does explain why they never mix up 'if' and 'when'. For Dutch speakers, the best advice is to act as if the more ambiguous word *als* does not exist. When speaking English, it is easier to decide where to use the old-fashioned *indien* (if) and where to opt for *wanneer* (when).

Small words: 'a' versus 'an'

Two of the most basic words in the English language are the indefinite articles 'a' and 'an'. Unlike Dutch, which relies on just one indefinite article *een*, English complicates matters by having two. The difference – as most people were taught at school – is that 'a' comes before nouns that begin with a consonant (*medeklinker*) and 'an' before a vowel (*klinker*).

But if this is the case, why do we say 'Sally earned an MBA at Harvard' but 'John is working towards a master's degree at Stanford'? Both words begin with 'm', don't they, so shouldn't both sentences take 'a'?

The choice between 'a' and 'an' is governed not by whether the next word begins with a consonant or vowel, as you may have thought, but by whether the next sound is that of a consonant or a vowel.

The 'm' in master's degree starts with a consonant sound. But, surprisingly perhaps, the 'm' in MBA begins with a vowel. (Sound it out in your head and you'll hear yourself saying 'em'.)

To use 'a' and 'an' properly, then, you need to get used to conducting a quick test of consonant and vowel sounds. This can get particularly complicated when words or acronyms begin with the letters f, h, l, m, n, s, and x, each of which can sound like a consonant or a vowel, depending on the word.

A good case in point are words beginning with an initial 'h'. We say 'a history degree' but 'an honorary degree' because the 'h' in honorary is silent, producing an initial 'o' sound.

It is not just consonants that can trip you up because they have a vowel sound. The reverse is also possible. Consider these two sentences: 'Procter & Gamble has a one-tier board' and 'Shell issued an ordinary share to every shareholder.' In 'one-tier board' the word one is actually pronounced 'won', accounting for the choice of 'a' over 'an'.

This distinction makes English devilishly complex. If you're confused about whether to use 'a' or 'an' in conversation and you don't have time to conduct the sound test, just slur over the indefinite article and hope nobody notices. But when writing, take the time to pronounce the nouns in your head before you commit yourself to either 'a' or 'an' on paper.

Small words: prepositions

Besides 'if', 'a' and 'an', there is a whole other category of deceptive words: prepositions. These words, used to indicate location in phrases and sentences, are troublesome in just about every European language. In some languages, such as German, the problem is compounded by the fact that different prepositions take different cases. Every generation, students of German are therefore required to learn *aus*, *bei*, *mit* etc as if their lives depended on it.

English prepositions are very difficult, not least for Dutch speakers who will find that certain prepositions sometimes are, and sometimes are not, literal translations of the words that you're used to. Learning Dutch, I ran into the same problem in reverse. In the beginning, I would say things like *ik zit op de telefoon* ('I'm on the telephone') and *ik doe mijn bril aan* ('I'm putting on my glasses'). General hilarity would then follow.

For Dutch speakers, three common expressions containing prepositions are particularly tricky because in English they deviate from what you have come to expect. Correct these three and you will end up eliminating a large chunk of mistakes from your linguistic repertoire.

1. **Welcome *in*.** I've lost count of the number of times I've seen and heard this mistake. In English you always welcome

somebody *to* somewhere and never *in*, as you would expect from your knowledge of Dutch. Even the most expensively produced tourist brochures will blunder and welcome foreigners 'in' the Netherlands. The error is all the more noticeable because it's something you say or write at the very beginning of your presentation or text. If you're not careful and don't remember to say welcome *to*, it will be all downhill from there. (While you're at it, please do not compound the problem by spelling welcome as 'wellcome'.)

2. **Congratulate *with*.** Never, ever congratulate somebody *with* something. The only correct way of conveying best wishes is to congratulate a colleague *on* the birth of a child or on being awarded a prestigious prize. Look closely (*con*gratulate/*on*) and you'll discover an easy way to remember the right preposition.

3. **Interested *to*.** Don't buy this book if you're interested *to* learn to speak proper English. But please do so if you're interested *in* learning proper English. Remember this particular rule by noting that the first two letters of 'interested' provide a clue to the right prepositional phrase (*in*terested/*in*).

Other prepositional phrases to watch out for and to learn by heart, either because they are so common or because they are different from what you might think:

at a loss	not sure what to do
at short notice	with very little warning
behind schedule	running late
win **by** default	succeed due to lack of competition
from scratch	with nothing prepared or organized beforehand
in depth/**in** detail	thoroughly
in retrospect	in hindsight (*bij nader inzien*), looking back
off the record	not for publication
on condition that	provided that
with ease	easily
goes **without** saying	is obvious

Prepositions and other little words are what make languages fun and challenging. Unfortunately, they are also the ultimate test of your knowledge. A spell-check will not pick up on these mistakes but a native English speaker listening to you talk certainly will.

Small words: the ones even the natives get wrong

So far we've looked at short words ('if', 'an' and prepositions) which native speakers of English manage to get right most of the time. When in doubt, they rely on their ear and linguistic instincts.

However, there are also short words that even the natives get wrong. A good example is 'a lot'. It's important to remember that this 'word' is actually two words and should always be spelled as such. 'Alot' is wrong, however often you may see it spelled incorrectly. (Don't worry if you come across 'allot'. This is a legitimate word meaning *toewijzen*.)

Another classic mistake is to confuse 'till', 'until' and ''til'. These three are all used to say the same thing, but only two of them are actual words in English. The third is a common bastardization that you should learn to avoid.

Most people think that 'until' is the original word and that 'till' and ''til' are interchangeable abbreviations. The truth is that 'till' is the older word by far, with a history stretching back to the 9th century when it simply meant 'to'. In the 12th century 'till' came to mean 'up to'. A century later, the word 'until' was also somehow spawned, though it is highly redundant. Why? Because the prefix 'un' (derived from the Old Norse *und*) also meant 'up to', creating a word meaning 'up to up to'.

Language purists will therefore tell you that only 'till' and 'until' are acceptable, while ''til' is just plain wrong. My advice is: stick to 'until' in all instances, even though it's slightly longer (and redundant if you know your Old Norse). Using 'till' might tempt you to make the mistake of writing ''til' and before you know it you'll even succumb to ''till', the most dreaded error of all.

Another small word which native English speakers manage to mangle is 'as'. Far too often they use the word 'like' where 'as' or 'as if' is called for. Mimic the natives around you and you'll be led into a grammatical wilderness. Here are two examples of incorrect and correct usage of this common word:
- 'Net profit has not risen like we had predicted.' (wrong)
- 'Profit growth has taken off like a rocket.' (right)

In the first sentence, the speaker should have said: 'Net profit has not risen as we had predicted.' Why? The conjunction (*voegwoord*) 'as' is needed whenever you introduce a clause (*bijzin*) containing a subject and a verb, whether it is stated outright or merely implied. In the second sentence, by contrast, 'like' is a preposition (*voorzetsel*), meaning that the word that follows must be a noun, not a verb.

Confused? You are not alone. English does contain some famous lines in which correct grammar is beautifully illustrated, as in: 'When in Rome, do as the Romans do.' Most of the time, however, the rules are broken quite brazenly, as in:
- 'Tell it like it is.'
- 'I remember it like it was yesterday.' (Correct usage would be '...as if it were yesterday'.)
- 'Winston tastes good like a cigarette should.' (Famous advertising slogan from the 1950s to early 1970s that annoyed grammar lovers because proper English calls for 'as a cigarette should'.)

The Winston ad proved to be so offensive to language purists that the manufacturer delighted in provoking them further, coming up with the subsequent slogan 'What do you want, good grammar or good taste?'

Native English speakers are so afraid of using the word 'like' wrongly that they stop using it altogether as a preposition, substituting 'such as' and 'as with' instead, producing wordy prose. Try not to do this. One word is always better than two, except when it is a long one, as we shall see below.

Like wow

'Like' is a perfectly acceptable word except when it is used as an irritating interjection in everyday speech:

'It was, like, the best apple pie I've ever tasted. The crust was, like, really crisp, and the bits of apples tasted like amazing. I was like wow!'

Unless you're a teenager from Los Angeles (and even if you are), you don't want to sound like one. This overuse of 'like' as a meaningless filler is a key feature of 'Valspeak', the language of teenage girls in California's San Fernando Valley that has now spread worldwide. These Valley girls have also popularized two other words that are bound to irritate parents everywhere: 'Duh!' and 'whatever...' Join company with them and it's, like, end of story as far as your English goes.

Big words

The Dutch speaker is tempted to make long words even longer than they should be in English because of the Dutch language's fondness for stringing together words to create new and bigger ones.

My favorite word in Dutch has to be *hottentottententententoonstelling*. It is a completely nonsensical word that has never come up in any normal conversation that I've ever had or expect to have. But it is a wonderful illustration of the way that

Dutch can be adapted to create gigantic compound words (*samengestelde woorden*).

English is different. Where Dutch strings together nouns to create new nouns, English tends to keep them separate. So whereas the Dutch have no problem creating (and pronouncing) words like *televisieproductiemaatschappij*, English calls for three separate words: television production company.

The use of the butted compound (that is to say, the joining of words to form new ones) explains why words in Dutch are so long. Linguists have calculated that words in an average Dutch-language text contain 10.5 letters, as against 8.8 letters in English.

Why is this relevant? Because it illustrates a simple point. When writing in English you should immediately become suspicious whenever you find yourself writing down terribly long words. 'Managementteam', 'workpermits' and 'communicationskills' do not exist in English, though the separate words obviously do.

When in doubt, chop up those long Dutch-looking words. Be especially wary of two or more nouns stuck together. Chances are that they are meant to be separate words. And be aware (as is so often the case in English) that there are no hard and fast rules governing compounds.

 ## Supercalifragilisticexpialidocious

To be sure, English also boasts many extremely long words but most of them are nonsensical inventions, like the title of the song from 'Mary Poppins' above.

The writer James Joyce was also fond of inventing words in his novels. On the first page of *Finnegan's Wake* the unsuspecting reader is suddenly confronted with 'Bababadalgharaghtakam-minarronnkonnbronntonnerronntuonnthunntrovarrhounawn-skawntoohoohoordenenthurnuk'. This 100-letter word is Joyce's interpretation of the thunderclap that accompanied the fall of Adam and Eve in the garden of Eden.

Apart from a string of very long scientific and technical terms, there is one English word which, unlike *hottentottententententen-toonstelling*, was once actually used in everyday speech. The word 'antidisestablishmentarianism' describes the opposition movement which sprang up in 19th-century England to counter plans to separate church and state.

There is no reasonable explanation for why 'bathroom' should be one word but 'living room' two. Yet, if pressed, you can come up with a couple of obvious patterns. As a language, English seems happy to join up two words as long as they're short ('bath' and 'room'), preferably just one syllable each.

Secondly, over time, words will sometimes link up once they've firmly entered the mainstream of speech. In the early days of the computer era, people spoke of 'data bases'. Now, even the Oxford English Dictionary joins them up.

But the chance that 'computer' and 'screen', or 'computer' and 'network', will ever be merged is more remote, simply because the individual words are longer. I also think it's safe to say that we will never see 'Hottentot tent exhibit' become a single word.

My advice to Dutch speakers is therefore quite straightforward. As soon as you've typed eight letters in succession without a space, chances are that you're stringing together words illegally, at least as far as English is concerned.

Problem #3: verb tenses – the Dutch syndrome

Present tense

Before globalization you used to be able to tell nationalities apart by their shoes. If you looked at tourists lining up to enter St. Peter's in Vatican City, you could easily pick out the Americans (sneakers and white socks) and the French (sandals and blue socks) by their footwear.

Similarly, some nationalities can be distinguished by the mistakes they make in English. The Germans and Dutch, for instance, have quite deep-seated problems with the present tense – or with two of the present tenses, I should say.

English does not boast just one present tense but four:
simple present   (I work, or I do work)
present continuous   (I am working)
present perfect   (I have worked)
present perfect continuous   (I have been working)

The continuous tense presents the biggest difficulty for the Dutch. Basically, they overuse it, especially when talking about themselves.

'I am working for Shell for 10 years,' you'll hear a Dutch speaker say. 'I am living in The Hague, with my husband and two children. One of them is taking the bus to school, and the other is riding his bike.'

The -ing construction lies at the heart of the present continuous tense. Get it wrong or use it incorrectly, and you will have exposed yourself as a non-native speaker.

To avoid using the wrong present tense, first determine whether an action or an event is taking place **as you speak** or whether the action or event is part of a **recurring cycle or pattern**. Once you've determined the timing and regularity of the action that the verb describes, you can then choose the right verb without too much problem. The simple present covers all cycles and patterns, and the present continuous (in other words, the dreaded -ing construction) is reserved for things happening at that very moment.

Sound difficult? It's not for a native speaker – it's ingrained – but it is quite a challenge for Dutch speakers. In the case of your work or your career, you almost always need to resort to the simple present. But if you're describing what you're doing on a specific working day, then the present continuous may be called for.

Here are some examples that should help to clear up the mystery of the present tense:

Simple present

- '**I work** for Shell.' (in the sense that you've worked there since graduating from university)
- '**I drive** my car to the office.' (in the sense of an everyday occurrence, like traffic jams)
- '**I live** in New York.' (and have done so since 1990)

You can certainly use these same verbs or sentences with -ing but only if there is a sense of immediacy, which in turn requires the present continuous.

Present continuous

- 'Thanks for calling, but **I am working** late on the Shell deal tonight. Can I call you back?'
- '**I am driving** to the office right now, so please wait until I get there.'
- 'At the moment **I am living** in New York but I hope to move on next year.'

Once you have the present tense under your belt, it's time to focus on the next level of difficulty – the complication caused by adding the word 'since' to your sentences. The perfectly good Dutch sentence *Ik werk sinds 2000 bij Shell* should never be translated literally into 'I work for Shell since 2000', which Dutch speakers do all the time.

The addition of the word 'since' changes the sense of time and requires you to use either one of the two remaining types of present tense. The ominous-sounding present perfect continuous produces 'I have been working for Shell since 2000.' But in all instances the present perfect would also cover the situation, as in 'I have worked for Shell since 2000.'

To sum up, the present tense in English is anything but simple. Most of the time, when it comes to talking about your job, your family or where you live, translate literally from the Dutch because this will send you into the simple present (*ik fiets altijd naar mijn werk* becomes 'I always bicycle to work'). This is one of those occasions when a straightforward translation will do the trick. Enjoy it while it lasts, as it is not often that a word-for-word translation actually works, especially not in the future tense.

Future

I don't have statistics to back up my claim, but I'm pretty certain that the Dutch run into their greatest difficulties with the future tense at the end of a conversation, not at the beginning. They do perfectly well until the final sentence is uttered. Then they go wrong. 'I fax you the information tomorrow', you'll hear. Or: 'I call you next week.'

What the Dutch speaker has tried to do is form the future tense by translating literally from the Dutch (*Ik bel je volgende week.*) In most cases, this will not work because English requires the auxiliary, or helping, verb 'will' to indicate the future tense. Alternatively, the construction 'going to' may also work. So the correct sentence will be either 'I will call you tomorrow' or 'I'm going to try it again next week', depending on the context.

Why is it so easy to make this mistake, even for educated Dutch speakers? Perhaps we can pin the blame on the use of contractions (*samenvoegingen*) in everyday English speech. If you hear 'I'll', 'you'll' or 'we'll' said fast and often enough, the word 'will' gets slurred over, leading the Dutch speaker to leave out the future tense altogether. Or perhaps the real cause of the problem is simply that the Dutch are tempted to translate literally from their own language.

Either way, the result is pidgin English that sounds as if it's been lifted from an old John Wayne movie. Actors playing Indians (Native Americans!) may be forgiven for saying 'I go tomorrow to Big Chief.' Dutch speakers who want to come across as native English speakers will not.

By now, you'd be surprised – and perhaps also a bit disappointed – if there weren't any exceptions, and of course there are. When a clause (*bijzin*) begins with a time element such as 'when', 'while' or 'before', any construction involving 'will' in the clause is redundant. Therefore it's: 'When I see you next week, I'll hand you the report' because the future tense is already covered in I'll (I will). Dutch speakers, however, are tempted to use the future tense in the subordinate clause, too, producing errors like 'When I will see you next week, I will hand you the report.'

Finally, in older textbooks on English, the rules of grammar dictated that the auxiliary verb 'shall' be substituted for 'will' in the first person singular and plural. Strictly speaking, you should say 'I shall' and 'we shall' rather than 'I will' and 'we will', particularly if you wish to speak British English.

This construction is dying out, even in Great Britain, except in instances when a suggestion is being made as in 'Shall we go now?' or 'Shall we talk again next week about my pay raise?' And you also see 'shall' in legal documents, which still seem to exert endless influence on the English language.

Three cautionary examples

Let's face it, English is a difficult language to get right, however long you may have spoken it or however many books you might read on the subject. Native English speakers realize this and will make allowances for the inevitable blunders that creep into the speech of non-natives.

However, there is no excuse for bad English in the brochures, reports and signs that Dutch companies use to attract foreign customers. American and British executives would never trust their school French enough to allow a brochure to be printed and then sent to potential clients, based on what they learned about French grammar and vocabulary as 13-year-olds. Then why do the Dutch send badly translated English-language material into the marketplace?

The answer, as we saw in the first chapter, is that the Dutch are not perfectionists when it comes to language. Worse, they over-rate their English skills. They always manage to make themselves understood, so what's the problem?

The problem is that sloppy, often stilted English is immediately obvious to the native speaker. If you as a company or an organization can't be bothered to have the texts checked by a native speaker rather than by a secretary who spent a year as an au pair in London, then how committed are you to delivering outstanding service or products?

Here are three random samples of how not to present yourself in English. To protect the innocent or at any rate the naïve, I've deleted the names of the companies involved.

Example #1: at your service

Most hotels in the Netherlands do their best to help foreign guests find their way around the premises. Signs are generally bilingual and even multilingual, as are all menus and brochures.

Too often, though, the English-language texts have been written by a Dutch person who has not checked his or her work, and it shows.

A recent visit to a hotel near Utrecht uncovered a host of inaccuracies. The sign at the reception read 'Welcome *in* Hotel X' instead of *to*. The mistakes in English multiplied from there. The hotel's restaurant boasted 'original' Dutch cuisine. Real Dutch cooking is 'authentic', although certain individual dishes may well be made according to the original recipe.

The list of instructions in the event of an emergency (*hoe te handelen bij brand*) contained a whopper of a mistake: 'how to handle at a fire' instead of 'in the event of fire'.

At the reception, visitors were handed tokens to operate the automatic barriers located at the exit to the 'parking space'. What the hotel meant to say was 'parking lot' (American English) or 'car park' (British). A parking space is the rectangle in which individual cars are parked.

The point is not that somebody made a mistake in English. This happens to even the best non-native speakers of English, and to native speakers as well. What surprises me is that management will go to the trouble of printing an expensive brochure or menu – first hiring photographers, then lay-out people etc. – but not spend the extra money needed to hire a native speaker for the role of editor or translator.

There's a good English expression for this kind of *zuinigheid*: 'Penny wise, pound foolish.'

Example #2: so bad that it's almost good

Journalists are inundated with invitations to all sorts of events, many of them international. These English-language invitations are often a treasure chest of linguistic errors, but few can beat the one below for the sheer number of mistakes in just a few lines.

> '*Herewith* we cordially invite you *for* the opening of MUCH DUTCH, an official part of INSIDE DESIGN AMSTER-DAM 2006. It gives you an *inside in* the world of *dutch* design. *Showing new work of the best young designers we have in the Netherlands.* We are very proud to present designer [...] *Next to all that* Dutch Design we also *exhibit* the new work *of* [...], a very promising painter from Amsterdam *who's* work is inspired by [...]'

Where to begin? For a start, the English is mostly a literal translation from the Dutch, a method that is sure to produce big mistakes. 'Herewith' is a literal translation of *hierbij*, but this is unnecessary in the context. 'We cordially invite....' would have been fine on its own, except that you invite somebody *to* something, not for (*voor*). The phrase 'next to all that' is probably inspired by the Dutch *daarnaast*, whereas proper English calls for the phrase 'in addition'.

Then the other problems:
- 'inside' is a classic d/t problem carried over from Dutch into English. The correct word is 'insight' – and the correct preposition is 'into';

- the word 'dutch' is wrong if it is not capitalized;
- 'showing new work etc...' is a sentence fragment, not a complete sentence, and therefore out of place in a more formal text;
- '... new work of [...]' should be 'new work *by* [...]', a simple case of an erroneous preposition;
- the use of the present tense is also wrong in 'exhibit' – the sentence calls for the present continuous;
- 'who's' is a contraction meaning 'who is'. The word the author was looking for is 'whose' (*wiens*).

Example #3: grammatical therapy

These days, no self-respecting company can get by without a website. Most Dutch companies go one step further by providing an English site for foreign surfers on the web. That is all very well except when the English version is put together in a slapdash way, resulting in mistakes which unwittingly provide perfect illustrations of the lessons we've learned earlier in the book.

Let's take the example of a well-known men's retailer with stores at prestigious locations around the country, paying close attention to the verb tenses in the following quotes from the English-language web site.
- *Every day, when I'm walking on the Noordeinde towards the store, I feel proud.* This quote is non-native and therefore wrong. Given the regular pattern of the daily walk, the simple present is called for: '... when I *walk* along the Noordeinde to...'
- *For years X was dreaming of the highest attainable in his profession: an area to receive clients in total privacy and discretion.* As Mr. X has now realized his dream, the verb should reflect this accomplishment by switching to the past tense: 'For years X *dreamed* of ... in total privacy and *with* discretion.' (You receive someone with discretion, not in discretion.)

Throughout the website the word 'area' is used not only excessively but also imprecisely. In the quote above, it would have been better to say 'a place to receive clients', as an 'area' is anything but small and intimate. Similarly, the wording of the following sentence, which attempts to describe Amsterdam's P.C. Hooftstraat, is not completely right: *This street with its international air, is located in the middle of the famous Museum area.* Here, rather than saying 'area' the retailer should have chosen 'quarter', an upmarket way of saying neighborhood. 'International air' is also problematic, stemming as it probably does from a literal translation of *sfeer*. A better word would be 'ambiance' or even 'flavor'.

Two final problems on this website will suffice, I think. At a certain point the company says that its aim is to make customers *more aware of their personal presentation and the right click with the personality*. The company hopes to help the customer select clothes that suit him, that reflect his personality and that provide a good fit so that something clicks, or works. The use of 'click' in the original Dutch text does not work in English. If the author doesn't know what he or she means to say, how can the reader ever judge if this is the shop for him?

And here is how the owner allows himself to be described in English: *Rewarded with the Max Heymans Ring, an award for he or she who has made an important contribution to Dutch fashion.* This description is so ungrammatical that it detracts from the man's very considerable achievements. He was not 'rewarded with' the Max Heymans Ring, but 'awarded'. And this award 'goes to people who have made an important contribution to Dutch fashion', not 'for he or she', which is a multi-layered mistake. An award is presented *to* somebody, and the object of a preposition such as 'to' always takes the objective case (to him or her).

My point in sharing these three examples which have caught my eye in recent months is not to poke fun at mistakes. Rather than laughing I could cry when I come across linguistic lapses such as these, all of which could have easily been avoided. For the price of a suit in this famous retailer's shop, he could have had an English-language editor rework the language into proper native English, matching the care and expertise which the man unquestionably puts into producing his suits.

6. Numbers and squiggles

I vividly remember the first time I dreamed in Dutch. The dream itself I can't recall for the life of me. But what I do remember is my feeling of triumph. Entire snatches of conversation in that dream had taken place in Dutch, and I wasn't even awake! After 10 years of living in Amsterdam and speaking Dutch every day, and after reaching the ripe old age of 35, my subconscious had finally caught up and managed to produce a dream with a Dutch soundtrack.

Despite this achievement in the realm of words, I am still waiting – almost 15 years later – for that elusive moment when I will finally find myself mentally counting in Dutch. Numbers, it seems, are far more difficult to get right in a new language than you would think. Whenever I count coins in a shop or the number of knives needed for the dinner table, I know for a fact that my mind is saying 'one, two, three' and not *een, twee, drie.* What's worse, I think this will probably remain the case. My brain may form words in Dutch, even in my sleep, but numbers will stick in my mind in English no matter how long I live in the Netherlands.

My difficulty in counting in Dutch is a reminder that numbers, sizes, quantities and even the time of day are not as universal as they would seem. Culture and language have a way of influencing our grasp of numbers in ways that we are hardly aware of. Examples abound in everyday life but also in our historical consciousness. In the end, numbers can appear as foreign to people from other cultures as words can.

Triskaidekaphobia

As a group, Anglo-Saxons tend to suffer from superstitions far more than level-headed Dutch people. They are particularly prone to fear of the 'unlucky' number 13, known formally as triskaidekaphobia (from the Greek 'tris' = three, 'kai' = and, 'deka' = ten).

American hotels will skip the 13th floor, moving directly from the 12th to the 14th. And on most airlines, you'll search in vain for row 13.

Weights and measures

As a Europeanized American I am fairly adept at thinking metrically. I know that a heat wave is official once the temperature climbs into the 30s. I also know to start worrying about speeding tickets when the car's speedometer creeps past 120 kilometers per hour.

Your average American or, to a slightly lesser degree, average Briton is not used to thinking in terms of metric weights and measures. What's more, he never will be, at least not in our lifetimes. Although the metric system was successfully introduced into Canada in the 1970s and although most countries in the Commonwealth (the club of former British colonies) have gone metric, the United States and the United Kingdom continue to cling to their own weights and measures. The British government, however, does its best to promote the metric system alongside the 'native' version.

This stubborn attachment to the inch, foot and yard, and to the ounce, pound and gallon, is a reflection of the Anglo-Saxon's attachment to his own language. Yes, it is illogical and even ridiculous to force school children to spend years learning that 12 inches go into a foot; that three feet go into a yard; and that a mile is 5,280 feet long. And yes, it would be much more efficient to coerce the entire population of the US into learning the handy and foolproof metric system.

But just as lovers of the English language are downright proud of its idiosyncrasies and its refusal to bow to logic, so many English speakers revel in the curious inconsistency of their weights and measurement system and in the romance of its early roots. For instance, we owe the yard – a unit of measure that comes closest to the metric system's meter – to King Henry I (1068-1135). The yard was derived from measuring the space from the tip of his nose to the tip of the fingers of his outstretched arm.

Nearly a thousand years later, this odd unit of measure still underpins both the American and the British system. Yet other older units which were used in the intervening millennium have disappeared. The very small unit known as the grain (64.8 milligrams) is no longer in common use, nor is the drachm (1.771 grams). At the other end of the scale, the wonderfully named 'hogshead of beer' (equivalent to 63 gallons) and 'hogshead of wine' (54 gallons) are now, sadly, obsolete.

Though they may be united in their hatred of the metric system, Americans and Britons cannot, as usual, agree on any number of details when it comes to weights and measures. A US gallon is 20 percent smaller than the imperial gallon. And when Americans say a 'ton of coal', they mean a short ton, weighing 2,000 pounds, whereas the British are fans of the long ton (2,240 pounds), roughly the same weight as a metric ton.

But the biggest difference of all is that the British still weigh themselves in stones, an ancient unit of measure equal to 14 pounds or 6.35 kilos. Somebody who weighs 158 pounds (72 kilos) will say he or she weighs '11 stone 4' (meaning 11 stone and 4 pounds), or at least they will if they live in Britain or come from Britain. Notice that 'stone' is almost always used in the singular, even if the person in question is very heavy and weighs many stones indeed.

Even for Americans it is almost impossible to get used to thinking in terms of stones. When a British friend starts talking about an amount of weight lost or gained in stones, the best approach is to nod sagely, murmur appropriately and fight down any urge to translate the figure into kilos, pounds or any other known quantity.

 ## Spelling weights and measures

It's bad enough that the Yanks and the Brits can't agree on weights and measures. But they also disagree on how to spell them.

Those Americans who know and use the metric system write 'liters' while their British cousins spell it 'litres'. The same goes for ton, gram and kilometer (American) and tonne, gramme and kilometre (British).

Time of day

The Dutch and other Continentals are so used to making appointments for *19.30 uur* and *23.45 uur* that they don't realize how odd these times of day look to a pure-bred Anglo-Saxon, whether he or she lives in America or New Zealand. In the English-speaking mind, the 24-hour clock is reserved for soldiers, spies and astronauts – anybody, that is, who is forced to operate in a hierarchical world.

For business appointments but also for social occasions or any other scheduled time, stick to the two 12-hour cycles which are still in vogue in English-speaking countries. Anything from midnight to noon is a.m. (from the Latin *ante meridiem* for 'before midday'). After noon and up to midnight, the designation p.m. (*post meridiem*) is used. So your breakfast appointment for *8.30 uur* becomes 8:30 a.m. while dinner at *19.30 uur* is served at 7:30 p.m. (Eagle-eyed readers will have spotted that English uses the colon, or *dubbele punt*, to separate the hours from the minutes, a small but necessary change from the period used in Continental countries and elsewhere.)

Non-natives will sometimes scoff at the 12-hour clock, saying that it is imprecise and impractical. In fact, their dismissal of this quaint but annoying tradition is not unlike their lack of understanding for the very real fondness which your average Anglo-Saxon feels for his weights and measures. Grams, liters and 24-hour designations of time may be more logical but you are missing the point if you don't 'get' the native's point of view.

Dates

The shocking events of September 11, 2001 have already gone down in history as '9/11'. The terrorist attacks on the World Trade Center in New York and on the Pentagon have entered the world's collective mind in American shorthand for this historic date. The term is now so familiar and so widespread that it is easy to forget that before the attacks '9/11' to most people simply stood for November 9.

In linguistic terms, the attacks on the US have brought home to the rest of the world that Americans adhere to a mm/dd/yyyy format when it comes to dates. Their British cousins prefer dd/mm/yyyy, as do most Continentals and the Dutch. (To make matters even worse, many Asians put the year first, producing a yyyy/mm/dd pattern.) To avoid confusion, it is always best to write out dates in full and forego shorthand such as 02-03, which could be either February 3 or March 2, depending on which side of the Atlantic the person reading your texts calls home.

Another common 'mistake' is to use one's date of birth to signify age. In a Dutch text it is perfectly acceptable to refer to 'Ruud Lubbers (1939)' or 'Ruud Lubbers (Rotterdam, 1939)'. To an Anglo-Saxon, the date of birth as indicator of age stands out as funnily foreign, though the sense is clear enough, especially as the internet encyclopedia Wikipedia has adopted this habit. If you wish to give your texts a properly English flavor, however, there's no alternative but to write 'Ruud Lubbers, 68'.

Once the person in question is dead, it suddenly becomes perfectly all right in English to include the year of birth, and of death, after his name. For this reason you should not be surprised to see 'William Shakespeare (1564-1616)' but you'll never see 'Tony Blair (1953)' until after he has departed this life.

Telephone numbers

Recently, when I telephoned the call center of a Dutch company to ask about a bill, the voice-activated computer asked me to say my postcode not only slowly and clearly but also in a set pattern. The postcode 1234 could be given only as 'twelve, thirty-four'. In the Dutch context this is utterly sensible and logical. But if you are dealing with Anglo-Saxons, you should know that, to them, numbers do not come in pairs but in a string. This fictitious postcode would therefore be dictated as one-two-three-four.

Telephone numbers are equally culture-bound. To the Dutch eye, a telephone number like 00-31-70-22-33-444 is easily understood and quickly dialled. An American or a Briton would never divide the numbers up in pairs in this Continental way. For a local telephone number in the United States, the most common pattern is the first three numbers and then the remaining four, producing something along the lines of 222-3333. When you add an area code for a region, you end up with 111-222-3333.

This may seem a piddling point but it isn't really if you're about to spend thousands of euros on new business cards or office stationery. If your business involves lots of overseas contact with Americans, for instance, you might just want to array your telephone number in a way that will seem more familiar to them.

Which floor, please?

Say 'first floor' in America or Britain and you're liable to get very difference responses.

Britain and most of its former colonies (except the US, most of Canada and Singapore) follow the Continental example and call the ground level of a building the 'ground floor'. The next floor up is the first floor, and this system continues upward (though some buildings may skip the 13th floor).

To North Americans (except Quebec, which adheres to the European system) the ground floor is the first floor. From here on up, the two systems remain one number out of sync: a European's first floor is a North American's second floor, etc.

Big numbers

Getting a telephone number or a floor wrong is not the end of the world, of course. But you really have a problem on your hands if you mix up big numbers, especially truly huge numbers that run into the millions, billions and trillions.

Up until the million mark, the Dutch, British and American systems of numbers are alike – ten thousand is the same as *tienduizend*, one hundred thousand is *honderdduizend* and so on.

The headaches start after that. The next step up from million in English is billion. The Dutch equivalent is *miljard* but many Dutch speakers are tempted to say *biljoen*, mainly because it looks so similar. But beware: the word *biljoen* doesn't mean billion in English but trillion. Once again, you need to proceed with care because, although *triljoen* is a perfectly good Dutch word, it doesn't mean the same as an Anglo-Saxon trillion: the proper translation of *triljoen* is quintillion.

The problem is compounded because (true to form) even Anglo-Saxons themselves do not agree entirely on the right terms for really big numbers. In traditional British English, a billion is a numeral 1 followed by 12 zeros. An American will insist that a billion is followed by nine zeros.

If by now you're confused, don't worry: you're in good company. Even the best and brightest of financial journalists mix up their billions and *biljoenen*, which is a bit of a problem because the difference between the two – about three zeros – is immense, especially when we're talking dirty, hard cash.

The problem with zeros is that such large numbers (and, by extension in the business world, such huge amounts of money) are simply mind-boggling. Given that few of us have ever seen a billion dollars or a billion euros, the concept remains elusive. If you as a Dutch speaker wish to keep your billions and trillions in English straight, here's a handy guide:

Dutch	American	zeros
miljoen	million	six
miljard	billion	nine
biljoen	trillion	12
biljard	quadrillion	15
triljoen	quintillion	18

A bit of memorization will, as always, go a long way. But it doesn't explain why and when the Dutch and the American systems of counting large numbers diverged so radically. The people to blame are the French (a favorite pastime of both the Americans and the British).

The French were the first to devise a way of handling huge numbers. Back in the 15th century they came up with a system of categorizing numbers larger than a million, based on huge steps of a million at a time. Under this system, a billion – the next step up – was another way of saying 'a million million', meaning a number with 12 zeros. This is the origin of *biljoen* in Dutch and billion in British English.

The system worked perfectly well until the 17th century, when the French decided that increments of a million were too large. They then decreed that the leap from million to billion, and from billion to trillion, should be 1,000 times the previous one, not a million times. This revised French system was exported to the New World, explaining why today's American billion has 'just' nine zeros.

Having imposed this new system on the colonies, the French decided much later to go back to the original 15th-century definitions. The rest of Europe and Britain followed suit, leaving a gulf between American and European usage of these mind-boggling, big numbers.

But where does this leave the Dutch speaker eager to learn proper English? Do you adopt American English when it comes to the word billion, or do you opt for the British definition?

In practice, American definitions have eclipsed traditional British ones, even in the United Kingdom. The muscle of Wall Street and the power of the America economy have meant that the American sense of million, billion, trillion has emerged victorious, at least in the English-speaking world. So even if you decide to adopt British English rather than American, you'd probably be better off getting used to American terminology for big numbers. This is especially true if you're an accountant or a stockbroker, because any confusion could lead to huge losses and irreparable harm to your reputation.

 ### Oodles of zillions

Numbers like millions, billions and trillions are needed whenever you get down to serious business. But there are also more informal circumstances when you want a word for a huge amount without having to be too precise.

Informal English has a number of terms for indeterminately large amounts. These are all linguistic constructs bearing no relation at all to real numbers.

When amounts get big, then huge and finally humongous, you talk of 'zillions', 'gazillions' and even (though less common) 'jillions', following the model of million, billion, trillion.

Another way to conjure up images of gigantic amounts is to say 'oodles of' something or 'a slew of' something else. These nonsensical words are anything but precise but they sometimes fit the bill, as in 'I have oodles of time' or 'I've got a zillion things to do today.'

Small numbers can be equally troublesome. The problem is that decimals in Dutch take a comma, whereas a period (or full stop in British English) is called for in English. This means that a copy of *Het Financieele Dagblad* costs 2,00 euros in Dutch but 2.00 euros in English.

The same is true for somewhat larger numbers. The Dutch use dots where English speakers use commas, and vice versa. Had the famous us game show of the 1950s, 'The $64,000 Question', ever been aired in the Netherlands, its name would have had to be changed to 'The $64.000 Question'.

Counting and grammar

English is a peculiar language in the sense that you can't really speak it properly unless you have learned to count. Quite a few essential points of grammar rely on your being able to distinguish between things that can be counted and those that cannot.

This is a challenge even for Anglo-Saxons, as a trip to any American supermarket will soon reveal. The problem from a linguistic point of view is not just the spelling on the packaging of the products on display, though this is bad enough ('lo-calorie', 'hi-fiber', 'cheez'). The real killer is the express checkout lane. There, to the dismay of lovers of English, can usually be found an annoying sign that reads '10 items or less'.

Unlike Dutch, English requires that you know how to count in order to differentiate between words like 'many' and 'much' or 'fewer' and 'less'. In the case of the checkout lane at the supermarket, the sign should properly read '10 items or fewer'.

For the non-native speaker it's all a bit confusing. Why do you say 'so much food' but 'so many sandwiches'? Similarly, what is the rationale behind 'less information' and 'fewer books'? In Dutch you can get by with just *veel* or *minder*.

The difference lies in the nature of the noun. Some nouns are countable in the plural (for example, ten sandwiches, or one hundred sandwiches, or even a thousand sandwiches). These are count nouns. Others, by contrast, are considered to be mass nouns because they refer to a single whole. In your mind's eye, you see the collective rather than the individual entities.

In practice, mass nouns are the more difficult of the two types. Mass nouns fall into categories such as abstractions (management, love), natural occurrences (thunder) and things made up of thousands upon thousands of smaller parts (rice, sand, grain).

You can't divide up 'love' or 'gratitude' into smaller bits. So these are mass nouns. But you can count up the number of kisses, or the amount of thank-you notes you have written. These are count nouns.

A simple test is to ask yourself whether you can add an -s or -es at the end of the word to form a plural, or whether it sounds funny when you tack on the article 'a' or 'an' before the noun. Try this with 'love' and 'kiss' and you'll see what I mean.

If you can't form a singular or a plural, you're dealing with a mass noun. This, in turn, means that you need to use 'much' (not 'many') and 'less' (not 'fewer'). To return to the supermarket for a moment, you can now see why the sign should say '10 items or fewer' because 'item' is a countable entity.

Be aware, though, that some nouns such as 'time' can go either way. Compare 'How many times have I told you to write that report?' with 'How much time do you need to finish the business plan?'

Basically, then, you need to start counting when you're faced with the dilemma of choosing between 'many/much' and 'less/fewer'. Above all, count your blessings that Dutch is, relatively speaking, so much more straightforward than English.

Count nouns and mass nouns are also responsible for a major difference between British and American English. In *The Times* of London it is perfectly normal to read articles that begin 'Football club Arsenal have won ...'. The same story in *The New York Times* would begin 'Soccer team Arsenal has won ...'.

What is important about these two sentences is not that Americans say soccer where the British say football, but that the British newspaper has given Arsenal a plural verb, while the American paper has opted for a singular verb.

What is going on here? In most languages, you can be sure that a singular noun always takes a singular verb (*ik vlieg morgen naar Londen*) and a plural noun a plural verb (*wij vliegen*). English, of course, has to be different. For complex reasons that have to do with counting, British and American English diverge on this essential point of grammar.

Because some concepts can't be broken down into constituent parts and others can, British English applies this distinction to the noun-verb relationship. The problem arises all the time, not just in sports but also particularly in the world of business. Consider the following sentence: 'Management have this afternoon decided to fire half the workforce.' Again, the use of 'have' is a clear sign that this draconian measure was devised in London, not New York, because an American would say 'management has decided'.

Besides the word 'management', you run into the same American-British divide with other singular nouns such as team, working group, committee and so on. In American English, these single nouns invariably take a single verb. In British English, they can take either a singular or plural verb, depending on the circumstances.

In the sentence 'The inter-departmental team are aware of their responsibilities', the word team clearly refers to a group of individuals, explaining the British use of 'are'. But a British colleague might then go on to say: 'The inter-departmental team is ready to deliver its final report.' Here, the team is a single-minded body, therefore requiring a singular verb.

So how should you, as a Dutch speaker, deal with this tricky problem? If you work in a predominantly British setting, learn to distinguish between the collective and its individual members and then vary your verbs accordingly. In other cases, use American English – it's simply easier.

When all else fails, rewrite the sentence. 'Members of the management board have sacked half the company' gets you around the problem. Luckily, you'll be pleased to learn, a plural noun always takes a plural verb, in all varieties of English.

Counting and individual words

Understanding the difference between count and mass nouns will also help you to use the words 'amount' and 'number' correctly. As the word itself implies, 'number' can only be used with count nouns: 'a number of topics', 'a large number of caravans', 'a small number of terrorists'. By contrast, 'amount' is reserved for those indivisible mass nouns: 'an amount of money', 'a large amount of patience', 'a short amount of time'.

Similarly, the importance of counting crops up with the words 'between' and 'among'. Strictly speaking, the preposition 'between' is reserved for situations involving *two* people or things, while 'among' is used when the number involved is *three* or more; 'Jesus was forced to choose between Peter and Paul', yet 'He divided the loaf of bread among his 12 disciples.'

In practice, 'between' is used much more often in informal speech than 'among'. A mistake made in the use of 'between/among' is a far less serious offence than 'many/much' and 'fewer/less'. As always, it is wise to pick your battles, even when it comes to learning English.

Squiggles

Most of this chapter has been devoted to numbers, pure and simple, in telephone numbers, dates, systems of counting and as points of grammar. As we have seen, numbers create unexpected problems in English for Dutch speakers. For that reason, you'll be relieved to know that English has relatively few squiggles. By 'squiggles' I mean the various symbols that occur in texts alongside letters and numbers.

Dutch and German have umlauts as distinguishing squiggles, while French and Spanish have accent marks and cedillas. English has no native accent marks to speak of, except for those that accompany words which have been imported wholesale into the language, like café, touché etc.

Of course, there are plenty of punctuation marks in English – periods, commas, question marks and the like – but these are the same as the ones you are familiar with in Dutch. Unfortunately, the huge differences between Dutch and English grammar also influence the way punctuation marks are used in the two languages.

Life is too short for you to worry about all of them. But there is one squiggle on which you really do need to focus, and that's the apostrophe. In both English and Dutch, apostrophes are troublesome, but for very different reasons.

The apostrophe

Apostrophes in English are crucial in forming possessives (Tim's new job, or the marketing department's latest foul-up). However, as we saw in the section on spelling, they are never needed in English to form plurals except in very specific situations requiring visual clarity (d's and t's, p's and q's, pda's, cv's).

In Dutch, by contrast, they are clearly needed when the singular ends in -a, -i, -o, -u or -y. Otherwise, the plural would be pronounced incorrectly (think of the words *alibi's* or *hobby's*). So, not surprisingly, the urge to stick an apostrophe unnecessarily into the plural of English nouns is almost irresistible for many Dutch speakers.

If you enjoy your team at work, say that you're fond of your colleagues, not colleague's (in Dutch you'd say *één collega, twee collega's*). The same is true of all plural nouns.

Possessives are the real *raison d'être* for the much abused apostrophe. Confusingly, for both Dutch speakers and native English speakers, the apostrophe in possessive words can come before the 's' but sometimes also after it. In some texts you'll see a reference to 'the bird's beak' but later also to 'the birds' feathers'.

The easy explanation here is that 's is used to form the possessive of a singular noun (bird's), and s' is needed for plural nouns (birds').

This is all well and good but what do you do, for example, if a singular noun ends in -s, as in the case of Philips? The answer is that even a singular noun ending in -s takes 's (Philips's new cd-player, for example).

But there's another complication. The rule about plural nouns taking s' applies only to nouns that end in -s in the plural (readers', drivers'). Nouns that don't end in -s at all, like children, men and women, require 's, even though the noun is clearly plural (children's shoes, women's dresses).

Above all, remember that these rules apply to nouns only, and not to possessive pronouns. One of the biggest mistakes in English is to confuse 'its' and 'it's'. The word 'it's' is not a possessive but a contraction of 'it is'. Compare 'It's the economy, stupid' with 'The economy is at its peak.' Both statements may be true, but only one should include an apostrophe.

If you make a mistake, as you almost certainly will, do not despair. You will be in good company. Native speakers are forever using unnecessary apostrophes, too. These mistakes prompted the British columnist Lynne Truss to write *Eats, Shoots & Leaves: The Zero Tolerance Approach to Punctuation*. Three million copies later, she may be no closer to eradicating bad punctuation. But she's a sign of hope (and of commercial success) for language columnists everywhere.

Your signature

The dictionary defines a squiggle as a small, wiggly mark, which explains why I've used it to cover the seemingly trivial but oh-so-important apostrophe, a key ingredient in proper punctuation. But squiggle has a second meaning – an illegible scrawl – which brings me to the subject of signatures.

The Dutch signature as squiggle has intrigued me ever since my daughter Kate, now a teenager, was first learning how to write. Recessed deep within her brain and her Dutch genes was a desire to develop an illegible signature. From the age of six onwards, she delighted in practicing signing her name in a way that would stand her in good stead if she ever had to sign autographs as a famous Hollywood actress. Her signature today has a wonderful artistic flourish but is irreparably illegible.

In this way Kate is staying true to her Dutch roots, despite her having an American-born father. Dutch signatures are an artistic translation of one's name into lines and curves that are indecipherable to any and all outsiders. In most signatures you will not be able to separate out names that you'd recognize, such as Robert, Jan, Marijke or even the omnipresent 'van de'. Instead you are confronted with an imaginative line, a mysterious password, a scribble.

How different signatures work in English-speaking countries. If you 'google' the signatures of American or British dignitaries like Bill Clinton, George Bush, Tony Blair and Gordon Brown, you'll find that their names are, for the most part, legible. In English-speaking countries, signatures – while distinctive and individualistic – are mostly made of letters that you can read, not lines and flourishes that you admire.

The difference between Anglo-Saxon and Dutch culture on this point is to an extent a question of education. English-speaking children are taught to produce legible signatures. But there is a second explanation, one that is rooted in economic systems. At the consumer level, banking in America and Britain is still largely based on the personal check which people write out to each other, unlike the *acceptgirokaart* which is sent to the bank and not directly to the recipient. For this reason Anglo-Saxons may be more programmed to produce legible signatures because these are designed to be read in the first instance by other humans, not machines.

Whatever the reason, you'd do well to transform your squiggle into a fairly legible signature if you find yourself living or working in an English-speaking country. Otherwise it will simply scream 'non-native'.

7. Beyond Babel Fish

English can be an infuriating language. Just when you think that you've learned a useful rule or detected a helpful pattern, you find yourself confronting new difficulties and new exceptions. No wonder that most people, including native speakers, have a love-hate relationship with English. If the language weren't so useful, you might consider giving it up altogether and concentrating on another tongue, like Chinese for instance.

The frustration which everybody encounters with English at one point or another is a reflection of its complicated history and maddening structure. My basic message in writing this book has been to encourage the reader to appreciate the nuances of English rather than waste time wishing the language were more logical.

Nevertheless, every new generation has tried to reform English. The temptation to make it more logical is understandable. Equally unsurprising is that most attempts at reform have concentrated on spelling, arguably the most annoying part of the language. In the past, such towering figures as Noah Webster, Benjamin Franklin, George Bernard Shaw and Charles Darwin have all supported the idea of finding ways of spelling English words the way they sound. Today the hope of creating logical English spelling lives on in institutions like the Simplified Spelling Society, whose efforts to introduce spelling reforms began back in 1908.

The mission of spelling reformers has always been to re-establish the ties between the phonetics of English – the way that the language sounds – and the spelling of individual words. They sincerely believe that 'jeneral eduekaeshon kood be konsiderably impruuvd if konsistent sistemz ov riting langgwejez wer introduest'. In other words, 'general education could be considerably improved if consistent systems of writing languages were introduced'. Reformists dream of the day when we will write 'write' as 'rite', and that spellings such as 'nite', 'lite' and 'thru' will win wide-spread acceptance.

So far all such attempts have failed and for fairly simple reasons. First, there is no world body capable of enforcing new spelling rules. Secondly, no one strand of English is sufficiently dominant, meaning that it would be impossible for the Americans and the Brits, to name just two major players, to agree on a single system of spelling. And thirdly (and most importantly), English speakers themselves are – in a funny sort of way – attached to their weird language and its illogical spelling.

Yet every generation feels compelled to make another stab at changing English, and the current era of children reared on the internet is no exception. People learning English in the early 21st century have started to pin their hopes on technology. They hope that new gadgets and communication methods, like text messaging on their mobiles, will make it acceptable for them to lower their linguistic standards.

At the same time, today's students of English have a misguided hope that computer software and machines will make it easier to learn proper English. At the very least they expect that spell-checks on computers will find and correct their mistakes for them. But ultimately they await the day that translation from one language into another will be done by machines, and that they can continue to think in Dutch and have English produced for them by bits and bytes. This is what I like to call the Babel Fish fallacy.

Science fiction fans will recognize Babel Fish from *The Hitchhiker's Guide to the Galaxy*. Insert this species of fish in your ear and you are able to understand any spoken language instantly and effortlessly, thanks to Babel Fish's ability to sense the meaning of all words and sounds. The fish from Douglas Adams's book inspired AltaVista to name its online translation program for the internet Babel Fish.

In my view, there are three good reasons why new technology is not going to solve the English 'problem':

1. English remains a highly hierarchical language. Because language rules tend to get pretty relaxed in text messages (sms) and emails, it is more important than ever to know when to use formal language and proper spellings and when it is deemed appropriate to adopt the unauthorized spellings allowed in instant messaging. I'm afraid that no computer or computer program is going to help you make these key judgements.

2. English is rife with words that look alike but convey completely different meanings. A slip of the finger when typing can be fatal in English. You need to learn to distinguish among these words. The spell-check cannot do the job for you.

3. The prospect of fool-proof automatic translation as exemplified by Babel Fish is an illusion. Programs that claim to offer instant translations do little more than translate individual words, without reference to context or, more importantly, to culture. At the same time, many Dutch concepts cannot be translated neatly into English, and vice versa. Rather than pinning all one's hopes on computer programs, intelligent Dutch speakers would be far better off recognizing which words and concepts in English are culture-bound, and adapting their language accordingly.

Gadgets

Faith in a gadget-based future is similar to the belief people once had in the 'paperless' office. Remember the predictions made about the digital storage of information? In the new computer age, the theory went, people would no longer need to print anything out on paper because all the information you would ever need or want would be accessible on computers or computer networks. This new age has not come about and will not, simply because people feel the need for a paper-based back-up. If anything, more paper is being used (and wasted) than ever before, because the use of computers has created ever more documents which people feel the need to print out.

Claims for a gadget-based future are equally false, at least when it comes to English. Grammar, punctuation and vocabulary will all remain critically important to success in English, even in an age of instantaneous communication. You will still need to make distinctions between the formality of a proper letter to a court of law or prospective employer and the more playful mood of a text message. It's when you start signing off letters to your boss with a jaunty :-$ ('put your money where your mouth is'), as if you were chatting to him or her online, that you know you have gone too far.

In that respect, English is no different from any other language, even Dutch. However, English does observe one formality which Dutch has long since dropped, and that is the complete sentence. In English writing, it is considered bad form – and even impolite – to use sentences without a subject and a verb. Indeed, if you use a spell-check in English, the computer will flag these 'sentence fragments' and ask you to consider revising them.

In Dutch, however, sentence fragments are used all the time, even in more formal writing. Scan *de Volkskrant*, NRC *Handelsblad* and *Het Financieele Dagblad* and you will find examples on an almost daily basis. Both on inside pages and on the front page. And from time to time even in the lead paragraph of a news story. (These last two sentences are examples of fragments which are inappropriate in formal written English.)

The rule about complete sentences applies to most emails and certainly to those that are businesslike in nature, but not of course to chat or text messages. Use your common sense but be keenly aware that English is more formal in this regard.

You should also be sensitive to the fact that the emergence of gadgets like the mobile phone and pda's can adversely affect your linguistic judgement, particularly if you're a non-native speaker. The shrinking of computer screens to fit phones, plus the resulting reduction in the size of keyboards, has caused an explosive rise in the use of abbreviations and acronyms, most of which will be inappropriate in formal writing.

In English text messages it is not uncommon to come across acronyms like 'nbd' (no big deal), @TEOTD (at the end of the day) and F2F (face to face).

The danger of this development for you as a non-native speaker is that you may find yourself using these abbreviations in other forms of communication, too.

In business letters it is best to avoid abbreviations altogether. Emails, however, are a different story, as they occupy the middle ground between the breezy informality of a text message (which the Dutch and others call an *sms*) and the more studied prose of a letter.

So which abbreviations and acronyms are acceptable in emails to colleagues or clients? Quite a few are so commonplace that they can be used at will. These include FYI (for your information) and ASAP (as soon as possible).

At the same time, there are a host of abbreviations derived from Latin that are equally trouble-free: e.g. (for example), cf. (compared to), ca. (approximately), et al. (and other people) and, of course, the well-known etc.

In general, though, it is best in business correspondence to steer clear of abbreviations and acronyms, especially those that are either obscure or suggestive of the jocular tone of text messages.

In fact, as a non-native speaker you are almost always better off avoiding trendy new language and sticking to traditional words and texts wherever possible.

Spell-check

Your computer's spell-check can offer a bit of help when it comes to learning native English, but not that much in the end. As we have seen, one benefit of running an automatic spelling and grammatical scan of your writing is that the spell-check will pick out incomplete sentences and ask you to change them. In virtually every case, you would be well advised to do so.

But spelling is a different matter. The English language is filled with homonyms, or words that are spelled and pronounced alike but have different meanings ('bow' can mean a bend of the body or head, but also the forward part of a ship). Strictly speaking, some of the most difficult words are not homonyms, but homographs (words spelled alike but different in meaning or pronunciation) or homophones (words pronounced the same but different in meaning, derivation or spelling).

While Dutch is no stranger to *homoniemen* (think of the divergent senses of the word *bij* or *net*, for example), English will lead the unsuspecting non-native speaker into linguistic quicksand. Your spell-check will not detect this type of mistake for the simple reason that the 'incorrect' word is not wrong, but misplaced in that particular sentence.

To make matters worse, English is prone not just to homonym pairs but even to trios that sound the same but have different meanings. It is time, therefore, to look at the most common (and, by extension, troublesome) of these. But be warned: since you cannot rely on your spell-check, you'll need to memorize them (or resort to a dictionary) if you're really serious about learning to avoid them.

Double trouble

In Chapter 4 we encountered the difficulties the Dutch have with consonants that sound alike in their own language, causing them to treat certain pairs of words as homonyms in English when they are nothing of the kind (live and life, and send and sent, for example). They then go on to pronounce, spell and use them incorrectly.

But true homonyms in English are difficult for everybody, for natives and non-natives alike. A complete list would be just about endless.

Here are a few of my favorites, in no apparent order:

hoarse	a frog in one's throat (*hees*)
horse	animal beloved of pre-adolescent girls
bare	naked, empty
bear	animal, as in grizzly bear
pail	bucket
pale	light-colored
morning	the day up until noontime
mourning	sadness at the loss of a loved one
lessen	to reduce
lesson	instruction
guessed	past participle of guess
guest	visitor

cannon	large mounted gun that fires lead balls
canon	tenet of religious law, among other things
beach	area full of sand and tourists
beech	type of tree
dual	double
duel	ritualistic fight in the cause of love

Then there are the word pairs which are not really homonyms but confusing just the same. Get one letter wrong and you've committed quite an error:

beside	used mainly to indicate location (beside the garage)
besides	also, furthermore. ('Besides, I hadn't even had time to read the report.')
than	used in comparisons (bigger than...)
then	used sequentially ('I then called the office.')
effect	a noun: 'The effect of our cost-cutting drive was to raise profits by 100%.'
affect	a verb: 'News of the job losses affected him badly.'

advice/advise: 'Advice' is solely a noun, and 'advise' solely a verb. Once again, the Dutch get this wrong more often than native speakers because their pronunciation doesn't sufficiently distinguish between the c and the s.

practice/practise: The problem here is the Anglo-American divide. Americans use the 'c' in all instances. The British use 's' when the word is a verb (to practise the piano) and 'c' when it is a noun (a doctor's practice). The same is true of licence/license (see Chapter 2).

But there's good news when it comes to one pair: inquire/enquire. These have the same meaning – to ask – and are interchangeable. British speakers tend to use enquire (verb) and enquiry (noun) while Americans lean towards inquire and inquiry. However, both (you will be relieved to know) are correct, as are both pronunciations of the noun (INquiry and inQUIRY).

Your spell-check, then, cannot guarantee that you will be able to write like a native. A slip of the finger when typing can wind up dramatically changing the thrust of your text. Your computer will not be surprised to see 'mourning' rather than 'morning', but readers of the report on which you worked so hard certainly will be.

 ## Lost in space

Another keyboard disaster in English is the incorrect use of the space bar. If you accidentally (or even consciously) insert a space when typing certain words, you may wind up saying something you don't mean. The same is true if you forget to add a space where one is clearly needed. Let's look at some examples:

- 'Everyday' means daily, common, regular or ordinary, while 'every day' is another way of saying 'each day'. The proper use of these words produces sentences like 'I wear everyday clothes every day I possibly can.'
- 'Sometime' refers to an indefinite moment in the future, while 'some time' is more specific. If somebody tries to brush you off with a meaningless 'We must have lunch sometime', you can catch him or her off-guard by saying 'Shall I reserve some time for us on Thursday, then?'
- 'Everyone' is akin to 'everybody'. It applies universally: 'Everyone loves Kentucky Fried Chicken.' By contrast, 'every one' has a more focused range, as in 'Every one of the candidates for the marketing job turned out to be unsuitable.'

As a Dutch speaker, you could be at a real disadvantage on this score. By this I mean that you will probably tend to run words together anyway in English, reflecting the Dutch habit (discussed in Chapter 5) of forming *samengestelde woorden*, or compound words. The trick is to memorize the above and then to remember to use your computer's space bar wisely.

Triple threats

Of the confusing trios of English words that are pronounced alike yet have divergent meanings and spellings, three probably produce the most problems. Get these triple threats right and you will have infinitely improved your writing.

to	preposition indicating direction
too	informal way of saying 'also'; can also mean very, or extremely
two	number that follows one
by	preposition that can mean 'near' or 'toward'
bye	as in good-bye
buy	shop till you drop
their	plural possessive
there	location
they're	contraction of the words 'they are'

There are other instances when trouble really does come in threes. Consider these examples:

council	institutional body, such as a city council
counsel	another word for lawyer or attorney; advice; to advise
consul	diplomatic rank

carat (karat) unit of measure for gems and precious metals
caret proofreader's mark indicating where to insert a word
carrot vegetable beloved of rabbits

cite to quote somebody or something
site location, also on the worldwide web
sight something seen; ability to see

rain water that descends from the heavens
reign period of power of a king, queen or sovereign
rein to slow down horses, using reins (*teugels*); curb

vain full of oneself (*ijdel*); futile
vein blood vessel; rock seam; streak
vane a movable device indicating wind direction

poor without funds
pore very small opening in the skin
pour to decant liquid

palate roof of the mouth; an appreciation for taste
pallet portable platform for moving wood or other material; a straw bed
palette thin board on which to mix paints; small plate to protect armpits used in suit of armor

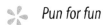 ## Pun for fun

On a lighter note, the homonym is the basis for countless English jokes using puns, or words that suggest multiple meanings. Especially in Britain, many people consider the pun to be an art form. To others, the pun is the lowest form of humor, eliciting groans and rolling eyeballs. You, the reader, can be the judge:

What do you call a murderer with fiber? A cereal killer
(a play on the words 'serial killer'; cereal is a breakfast food containing lots of fiber)

What did the fish say when he hit a concrete wall? Dam!
(a play on the homonyms dam, a water barrier, and the swear word damn)

Puns are probably a way for native English speakers to cope with the idiosyncracy, and even sheer idiocy, of their language. If you can learn to laugh at English, you're halfway to becoming a native yourself.

Translation traps

When it comes to expressions and sayings, word-for-word translations are no more helpful than your computer's spell-check in tackling the problems we have been describing. Whether you do these literal translations yourself or use computer programs such as Babel Fish, the end result is all too often a distorted version of the real message.

The Dutch, I would argue, are particularly prone to relying on simple translations when speaking English because of their practical approach to language. This attitude is best summed up by the view 'If people understand what I mean, then that's fine'. This is not fine at all, and for the following reasons.

First, literal translations produce inelegant language. Secondly, they frequently generate mistakes, because Dutch and English share words that can mean different things to different people. And lastly but most importantly, translations of individual words will never do justice to the cultural components of your message. Translations are fine up to a point, but to engage in intelligent discussion of certain subjects – school, politics, society – you need to understand that the world views of the Netherlands and of Anglo-Saxon countries are miles apart.

True translation is an art and, as such, cannot be left to computers, despite the very obvious advances that have been made. Years ago, when translation programs first came into vogue, everybody had fun translating well-known sayings from English into a second language and then re-translating the result back into English. A favorite example is 'The spirit is willing but the flesh is weak.' Translate this by computer into Spanish, and back again, and you get 'The alcohol was arranged but the meat was weak', while in Russian the result was 'The vodka was good but the meat was rotten.'

Things have moved on since then. But if you ask your computer to translate 'out of sight, out of mind' from the English, you still get *uit gezicht uit mening*, which is nowhere near acceptable.

Translating mechanically, then, is a sure-fire way of ensuring that you'll never speak proper English. To prove my point, I'll start with shorter words and expressions, but then end with concepts that are culture-bound. Why? Once you have learned that certain ideas simply can't be translated, you will be truly conscious of the need to speak to a native in his or her terms, and not in your own.

Faux amis

Because English and Dutch contain words that appear to be alike, Dutch speakers are easily lulled into thinking that these words mean the same in both languages. When this happens, linguists speak of 'false cognates', a phenomenon also known in French as 'faux amis'.

There are dozens of examples to choose from. The only way to avoid making these particular mistakes is to be so acutely aware of their existence that mental alarm bells go off whenever one of them comes up in conversation or in print.

- In English, a report which has yet to reach its final version is called a **draft** report, not a concept report (*conceptrapport*).
- If you need medicine your doctor will give you a **prescription**, not a recipe (*recept*). Recipes in English are limited to the kitchen except when used figuratively (a recipe for disaster, for instance).
- If you wish to convey that your statistics represent a *globale inschatting*, then you must fight the urge to say global estimate, which implies that your numbers are world-wide figures. The term you're looking for in English is **rough** estimate.
- The word map is a terrible trap for Dutch speakers. In English, it has only one meaning – that huge expanse of paper which helps you to get from A to B when you're on vacation and which is near-impossible to refold once you've reached your destination. In Dutch, *map* means the **folder** (or ringbinder if you work in an old-fashioned setting) in which you store paperwork.
- Managers (or parents for that matter) who are *consequent* in Dutch are **consistent** in English. 'Consequent' does exist in English (hence the confusion) but carries a different meaning, namely 'following as a logical outcome of earlier actions' (... the fraud he committed and his consequent dismissal).
- *Actueel* scores high on any list of common Dutch mistakes in English. The word you're looking for is **current** or **up to date**, depending on the context, and should not be confused with the word actual, which is a close equivalent of *feitelijk* in Dutch.
- In the same vein, *eventueel* seems designed to invite incorrect usage. The best approach is to use the word **possibly** instead, while keeping in mind that English contains a similar-looking archaic word, eventual, reserved for the discussion of something expected to occur at an indefinite point in the future (...the eventual collapse of civilization as we know it).

Word order

Words in isolation easily invite inappropriate translations, as the random examples above illustrate. But the same is true for phrases. In both short phrases and longer sentences, the Dutch have the tendency to impose their own sense of word order onto English, a habit that is exacerbated when you opt for word-for-word translations.

Again, a great many examples spring to mind but the most common, at least in the business and academic worlds, are the stock phrases commonly found in business or professional titles.

The problem is that so many Dutch job titles contain English words these days – marketing, deputy, sales, etc. – that you might think you can get away with translating the title on your Dutch business card and then simply transferring it to your English-language card and vice versa.

It is not uncommon to get business cards from Dutch people who describe themselves in English as 'manager international marketing & communications' or 'vice-president development and acquisitions'. Although such titles may look and sound like English, they're actually Dutch, at least when it comes to word order.

In English the modifier almost always (though wait for the exceptions below) comes before the noun it modifies. So if you've landed the job of 'international sales director', say so. Do not try to turn Dutch into English by saying that you're 'international director sales'. This is true of all such titles. If you call yourself 'interim marketing director', you've got the word order right. If you slip into Dutch and say 'interim director marketing', you have not.

If you can't kick the habit of Dutch word order, you can always inject the useful little word 'of' into your title. 'International director of sales' is, strictly speaking, not incorrect but it's much less common than 'international sales director'.

Inevitably, there are exceptions. In the fields of law and public administration, for example, titles such as 'director-general' or 'secretary-general' are not at all unusual.

These exceptions have a 940-year-old history dating back, as we saw in Chapter 5, to the Norman Conquest. The arrival of the Normans in 1066 ushered in three centuries of French ascendancy in English life and, inevitably, the English language. Until well into the 14th century, the language of the royal court and of the judicial courts was French, a language in which the modifier comes after the noun. This explains why, to this day, English-speakers say court martial and not martial court. In Britain itself, the final stage of divorce proceedings is still called the decree absolute, a French-influenced way of saying final decree.

But remember that these are exceptions which prove the rule that, in English, modifiers generally precede the noun. Failure to adhere to this rule will forever set you apart as a foreigner.

Far too often the Dutch speak stilted English because they translate sentences word by word, without bothering to rearrange them in the proper sequence. English has rules about word order, and it is important to learn them.

For foreigners learning Dutch or German, the problem is less acute because word order in these languages is so incredibly strict. A verbal element always comes second in any sentence, and all other verbs are then relegated to the back. More importantly, perhaps, we foreigners are then taught that elements of time always precede expressions of place: *Ik ga **morgen** naar **Londen***.

Once you've got that down, you can add manner: *Ik ga morgen **met het vliegtuig** naar Londen*. Put this all together and you have a rule that Anglo-Saxon speakers of Dutch often learn by heart: time-manner-place. I was taught to remember this by thinking 'TeMPo'.

By comparison, English is wonderfully free of rules – or so native speakers would have you believe. Sentence structure is looser, they'll say, and much less confining than in Dutch. This simply isn't true. In fact, the problem for Dutch speakers is that the underlying word order in English is opposite to the one they themselves take for granted.

So, if you're booked on a flight to Heathrow on Friday, you'll need to say: I'm flying to London tomorrow. In other words, in English the rule is 'Place Then Time'. Few native English speakers know that this rule even exists, let alone that there's a handy way for Dutch people to remember it: simply think PTT. Unfortunately, this helpful reminder will soon lose all meaning, as the good old postal service has now been renamed TNT. Let's hope that future generations will not be condemned to speaking bad English because a trusted institution has changed its name.

Cultural equivalents

All foreigners living in the Netherlands eventually realize that the word *gezellig* does not just mean 'cozy', as they were led to believe at first. It means many things, but mostly it conveys a sense of conviviality, of fun and good times. *Gezellig* is a shorthand term for anything that is social and positive.

Or so I thought until I found myself visiting my grandmother in The Hague one evening. Looking out the apartment window and spotting a yellow HTM tram trundling off into the distance, its interior lights ablaze, she murmured *gezellig* in complete delight at her daily view. Here was a new situation in which that most difficult of words was being used in a different way. The

Dutch language, which I felt I had just about mastered, was slowing slipping away from me once more.

The truth about Dutch, English and just about any language is that there will always be terms that can never be fully translated into a foreign tongue. The challenge for you as a Dutch speaker, or me as an English speaker, is to be aware of this and to become proficient at recognizing cultural differences. In an age when everything is supposedly going global, it is helpful and humbling to realize that many concepts are not very universal at all.

 ## Animal language

It's not just human language that defies translation. After twenty years in the Netherlands it still comes as a surprise to me that Dutch cows don't say moo, as they do in English, but *boe*. Horses in the Netherlands *hinnik*, whereas their Anglo-Saxon counterparts either neigh or whinny. And then there are cats. In English they purr, while in Dutch they *spin*.

Gezellig is a good example of a word that does not travel well from one culture to another. Rather than choosing one handy translation such as 'cozy' and automatically sticking to it, the foreigner in Holland is better off understanding the emotional force behind the word and then explaining rather than translating it. The same applies to the Dutch speaker who wishes to convey the notion of *gezelligheid* in English.

A similar approach is required for that most Dutch of words, *gunnen*. There is a simple, obvious translation when it comes to orders or contracts. These can be either 'awarded' or 'granted' (*gegund*). Unfortunately such a straightforward translation does not really do justice to the deeper reality that underlies the word. The useful expression *verkopen is gunnen* sums up the astute Dutch view that all business relations are based on personal relations, and that a deal is often the outcome of a complex weave of networks and mutual regard. *Gunnen* is a generous and magnanimous gesture, something which you bestow, like a favor, on a business partner.

In English, there is no good one-word equivalent for *gunnen* in this sense, so you need to devote many more words to the same message. 'Mark was well-disposed towards Jim and was happy to let him take credit for the deal' is probably the only way to convey *Mark gunde Jim alle lof voor de transactie*.

Funnily enough, the opposite of *gunnen*, or *misgunnen*, does have a perfectly good English equivalent: to begrudge someone something, as in 'Mark begrudged Tom his success in business.'

Another term that is completely culture-bound is the German-Dutch *streber*. It's hard in English to disparage someone who is excessively ambitious. Words like nerd, geek and brownnose are used to describe the intellectually ambitious but mostly in a school setting. Although you'll find it in the dictionary, 'striver' is a non-word. 'Careerist' or 'go-getter' doesn't carry the contempt of *streber*, and 'pushy' – which perhaps comes closest – is not a noun but an adjective. *Streber*, then, is essentially a word of disapproval that is closely linked to the *doe maar gewoon* mindset. As such, it only really makes sense in a Rhineland environment, making a proper translation all but impossible.

A final example (though there are so many others) of a Dutch word that doesn't work in English is *eigenwijs*. The difficulty here is that this Dutch word has perfectly acceptable, positive connotations, as in *Jantje is een heerlijk eigenwijs kind*. In English, all equivalent words are negative, such as 'pig-headed', 'stubborn', 'know-it-all', and 'smart aleck'.

In the case of *eigenwijs*, as is also true for words like *gezellig* and *streber*, the lack of an easy translation points to a huge cultural gap, one which the Dutch speaker (and the English speaker, for that matter) must keep in mind at all times. While Dutch parents like their children to be *eigenwijs* up to a point, parents in Anglo-Saxon countries prefer their children to be obedient. Understanding such differences is crucial if you are ever to find the words to express what you mean in English.

The list of words that don't translate into English is long and beyond the scope of this book. My goal is simply to warn the Dutch speaker against the mistaken assumption that certain ideas are universal and therefore easily translated into English.

Perhaps the biggest challenge facing Dutch speakers is finding a way to talk about the Netherlands' social and political structures in terms which native English speakers will understand. This is something I sensed but barely understood as a child.

Having spent all day at an American school with American friends and American teachers, I could not come home and talk about my experience in any other language than English. American high schools have home rooms, proms, study periods and all kinds of institutions which the Dutch language does not recognize. Conversely, my 13-year-old daughter Kate cannot really talk about the *brugklas*, her *mentor* or her choice between *athenaeum* and *gymnasium* in anything other than Dutch because the English equivalents of such words are so elusive.

For example, Dutch universities should not include in their English-language brochures information about their *studentenstop*. Using this Dutch word in English is pointless, although it happens all the time. Why? First of all, *studentstop* is not an English word. (The give-away is the fact that two words are stuck together, a common trait of Dutch but not of English.) Even worse, the very idea of a *studentstop* is alien to Anglo-Saxons and therefore to English. It would be unthinkable for prestigious universities in the US or the UK to allocate places by lottery. Instead, students compete with each other in the form of grades, essays and interviews to win a spot. May the best student prevail, not the luckiest: this is how their system works.

By the same token, the Dutch social security system, and even the Dutch world of business and work, are rife with terms that do not translate well into English, at least not directly.

To a Dutch person, using words like *inspraak* and *collectieve arbeidsovereenkomsten* and *arbeidsongeschikt* are second nature. To an English speaker, these terms are meaningless or at best vague. Rather than translating terms like *gezellig*, the Dutch speaker would do better to explain them, with particular reference to the Dutch culture from which they spring. There is no good equivalent for *arbeidsongeschikt*, for instance. In English you are forced to resort to 'disabled' or even 'incapacitated' yet these words will simply not do. They suggest a physical ailment and, as such, do not do justice to the WAO system. Many people receive this benefit because of a labor dispute, or due to psychological complaints, or because the WAO is (or was) sometimes used as a humane alternative to unemployment.

Related words that cannot be translated from the Dutch welfare system into an Anglo-Saxon world are *overspannen* and *overspannenheid*, a common ground for absenteeism from the Dutch workplace. English equivalents are far too heavy and dramatic. A 'mental breakdown' suggests admittance to a psychiatric hospital, while 'burn-out' implies a long course of treatment. The dictionary provides unhelpful translations such as 'overwrought', 'overstrung' or 'over-excited', none of which would be acceptable to an American boss when calling in sick.

Sociale partners also makes no sense when translated baldly as 'social partners'. Using this term for tripartite consultations among unions, employers and government – a cornerstone of the polder model – will draw a blank if you drop it into conversation.

So what do you say instead? There's simply no getting around it: you need to explain the system. And you will need to learn to choose your words carefully.

One more example will, I hope, clinch my case. You cannot in English say that you have 'a right' to five weeks of vacation a year (*ik heb recht op 25 vakantiedagen per jaar*). To an American in particular, this 'right' will seem peculiar, to say the least. A translation that would be a bit more acceptable is that you are 'entitled' to five weeks of vacation. But the bottom line is that, to an American, and particularly to an American employer, vacation is not a right but a privilege, one which can even be revoked if the pressures of work demand it.

The final test of your English extends beyond spelling, grammar, and your ability to cope with word order and numbers. The real challenge is to fit a 'cultural intelligence' filter onto your English, in the full expectation that the language which passes through it will be comprehensible to native English speakers everywhere.

8. Go Native or not?

While urging you to strive for native English, I have consciously stopped short of encouraging you to 'go native'. This quintessentially English term sounds positive but actually has negative connotations. It dates from the era of the British Empire, when a very small minority of administrators and civil servants who were sent to India or Burma adopted the new culture around them far too enthusiastically, at least from the point of view of their superiors in London. They took to wearing local costumes, to eating native foods and, most outrageously of all, to consorting with native women. In short, they went native.

To me, *Native English for Nederlanders* does not imply that the Dutch speaker should wear cowboy hats and learn to say 'howdy Ma'am' when speaking to a native or – at the other extreme – don bowler hats and an air of detached irony like a true Englishman.

On the contrary, Dutch speakers should do nothing of the sort. To speak proper English does not mean you have to renounce your Dutch personality. Indeed, why should you? The Dutch speaker's characteristic straightforwardness, for example, can be an asset in business – and in life generally – and should never be lost. For Dutch speakers, the challenge is not to renounce directness but to temper it. By understanding just how indirect native English speakers can be, the Dutch can choose to adapt their style, or not, according to time, place and circumstances.

Native English for Nederlanders encourages you to understand the native English speaker's language and, particularly, the culture behind it. My aim is not to create pseudo-Yanks or pseudo-Brits but to help you navigate the complexities and confusions of English, while ultimately remaining yourself.

Your goal should be to speak as much like the natives as you possibly can, without picking up their bad habits. Peppering your language with euphemisms, jargon or sports metaphors the way some natives do can be a big mistake. To communicate effectively you need to know that such linguistic tricks exist, and why. But understanding these habits is quite a different matter from parroting them yourself.

How do you guard against picking up mistakes along the way? First, be careful when copying the natives. Secondly, be wary of learning English from expats who have lived in the Netherlands far too long and whose language is now infected with 'Dutchisms'. And finally, don't repeat the mistakes your Dutch colleagues and friends may be making when they speak English. All in all, this is quite a tall order.

Don't mimic the natives

If we liken English to an intelligence test, it follows that few people manage to pass it with flying colors, not even the natives. Their English is often horrendous and full of errors. This should be a comfort, perhaps, but it makes you wonder what to imitate and what to avoid and how to tell the difference.

Sloppiness

As we have seen, English – more than most languages – is hierarchical. Written English reigns supreme at the top of the linguistic pyramid. Here it is important not only that your spelling be impeccable but also that you use complete sentences. Spoken English, particularly of the casual variety, is at the bottom of the pyramid. Here, almost anything goes, including swear words, which the Dutch tend to adopt far too readily.

Problems occur when the sloppiness of native English speakers spills over into the written language. All too often you will hear mistakes such as 'The test went real well' or 'I feel real bad about the mistake.' In both instances the speaker has neglected to say 'really well' or 'really bad', which is what proper grammar requires. The use of 'real' is wrong because these sentences require an adverb (*bijwoord*) and not an adjective (*bijvoeglijk naamwoord*). This basic error is even worse when it appears in black and white.

It is not just the grammar of casual everyday speech that the natives get wrong. Their pronunciation is often slurred and laid-back. Real problems arise if you incorporate these mistakes into your spelling.

The most blatant errors are easy to detect. You probably won't find yourself writing 'whaddja get' when you mean to ask 'what did you get?' The same holds true for other bastardized pronunciations ending in 'a': coulda, woulda, shoulda.

If you're not careful, however, sloppy day-to-day pronunciation and usage will affect your writing. The sentence 'We could of made more profit this year if the dollar had not dropped' looks all right at first, until you examine the grammar more closely. The correct verb is 'could have made', though you would never know it from the way people speak. The same danger lies in 'would of' (correct: would have), 'should of', etc.

These problems all stem from pronunciation that has gone wrong. It's only a small step from 'could have' to 'could've' to 'could of' and 'coulda'. Unfortunately, the only correct phrase is 'could have', which might come as a surprise if you're ever spent any time listening to taxi drivers in New York City.

The same phenomenon crops up in other situations, too. Based on how people speak, you might assume that it is correct to write 'You are suppose to submit your report in triplicate.' The correct phrase is 'supposed to', though the 'd' is silent in casual speech. Keep the same rule in mind with 'use to', a bastardization of 'used to'.

Finally, another common mistake, caused by the casual speech you hear all around you, is to write 'I will try and see whether I can arrange a meeting tomorrow.' The only proper way of writing this is to adhere to the more formal 'try to see'.

So sometimes when it comes to English the best advice is: write the language as it is meant to be written, not as it is spoken. This is not unlike the famous line that parents use in English when caught making a mistake they had warned their children about: 'Do as I say, not as I do.'

Hypercorrections

Besides sloppy pronunciation and run-of-the-mill grammatical mistakes, native speakers fall prey to what linguists call hypercorrections. A hypercorrection is a mistake caused by the fear of making a mistake and by the desire to sound educated and refined. In this sense, a hypercorrection is the opposite of sloppiness but equally wrong.

The temptation to use hypercorrections is present in all languages, including Dutch (the use of *hen* where *hun* will do, for example). In English, the biggest mistakes are made with 'whom' and variations of 'me'.

From a young age English speakers get drilled into them that they should never say 'You and me are going home'. Instead they need to avail themselves of the nominative case and say 'I' when speaking of themselves as the subject of a sentence.

This, in turn, leads to a fear of using the word 'me' in any compound, even when the objective case is clearly called for. Some

English speakers will therefore say things like 'Between you and I, the new boss is a bit of a bore.'

A very easy way to check this is to drop the compound ('and', 'or', 'between', etc.) – you will almost always choose the right word. For example, consider the sentence 'You and me are going home.' Drop the 'you and' and you'll quickly realize that you would never say 'Me going home'. This means that the correct phrase has to be 'You and I...'

Similarly, in the compound 'between you and I, the new boss is a real twit', all becomes clear if you drop 'between you' and recast the sentence: 'To **me**, the new boss ..'

In other instances, remember that the object of a preposition always takes the objective case 'me'. And do not, as English speakers sometimes do, try to avoid 'me' by using 'myself' instead ('Tom sent the report to myself and Sue.') 'Me', used correctly, is a perfectly good word and should not be feared. And remember to be humble and always put yourself last in these compounds ('... to Sue and me').

Like 'I', 'whom' is used incorrectly because people find grammar difficult but also because they fear sounding dumb if they mistakenly say 'who'.

The rule is fairly simple. 'Who', like 'I', is used as the subject of a sentence or clause. 'Whom' is the object of a sentence, clause or prepositional phrase. The same holds true for the words 'whoever' and 'whomever'. In the sentence 'Who gave it to whom?' both words are used correctly.

Problems arise in sentences such as 'Give the report to whoever answers the door.' You may be tempted to write 'whomever' because the word follows the preposition 'to'. But in this case the object of the preposition is the *entire* clause 'whoever answers the door', and 'whoever' is the subject of that clause and therefore used correctly.

If this seems confusing, you're in good company. Native speakers are forever getting this wrong.

Redundancy

English speakers have a predilection for redundancies. Redundancy occurs when words or ideas are repeated unnecessarily, producing woolly and wordy language. In everyday speech you will find redundancy in terms like little baby, evil villain, or new discovery. In each case the unnecessary adjective creates an annoying tautology.

Business English and the language of academia are both awash with redundant stock phrases. As a non-native speaker you will continually be tempted to absorb them into your own speech, especially if you hear them being used around you all the time. Once you are aware of them, however, you can start rooting them out and improving your English.

An 'end result', for instance, is no more final than a 'result'. By the same token, saying 'future prospects' or 'future plans' is inelegant because all prospects and plans lie, by definition, in the future.

Equally, an 'actual fact' carries no more weight than a fact on its own. And why say 'added bonus' when bonus already means 'something that is given in addition to what is strictly due'?

Above all, watch out for classic redundancies that begin with 're-'. These include such favorites as revert back, refer back, retreat back and so on. The prefix 're-' means back, so the extra use of the word is usually superfluous.

Similarly, there is a whole range of expressions that have redundant prepositions tacked on to them. These examples should all speak for themselves: gather together, combine together and delete out. Getting rid of extraneous words makes for strong, punchy texts. For this reason alone it is worth banishing them from your vocabulary.

Don't mimic the expats

At some point it happens to every native English speaker who lives in the Netherlands long enough, and it has certainly happened to me. All of a sudden I find myself asking my six-year-old daughter Ayat to 'turn the television softer' (*doe de televisie zachter*). What I mean to say, of course, is that she should turn the volume **down**. My English has become so infected by my Dutch that I sometimes end up speaking an odd mixture of the two.

When this occurs, you've been struck down by the Dunglish virus. Dunglish, an awkward mixture of English and Dutch, is a common affliction of the Dutch but even native English speakers are susceptible, provided that they have gone sufficiently native in the Netherlands. Unfortunately, the susceptibility of even the expat to an outbreak of Dunglish means that you can never be too careful when imitating those who should know better.

Avoiding Dunglish requires vigilance. It is a question of checking and double-checking prepositions and of rooting out the false friends we met earlier in the book.

In my experience Dutch managers and executives are the most liable to pick up bad habits. This happens because their professional language is full of English-sounding words which, when placed under the microscope, turn out not to be proper English at all.

Here are some of my favorite examples but there are obviously more. If you've been invited to a fancy office party in the evening, do not ask if you should wear a smoking. The proper term is 'black tie' or, in American English, 'tuxedo'.

The Dunglish word smoking is derived from smoking jacket, worn back in the days when the men retired after dinner to a separate room to puff cigars. In English, this meaning has been lost, so it's best to ban the word from your vocabulary, too.

Similarly, don't say you'll be out of the office next week because of a 'training'. No, you'll be away on a 'training course' or 'training program', when speaking British English. Americans will say that they're taking a course.

Another English-looking shortcut that doesn't work in English is holding. The proper term is a holding company. However, just to confuse things, there are times when the word holding on its own is perfectly legitimate: when your company owns shares in another company, that shareholding or *belang* is known simply as a 'holding'.

Outside the business world Dunglish confounds us in any number of day-to-day situations. A *valse hond* is not a 'false dog' but a vicious dog. An *ordinair meisje* is not an 'ordinary girl' (which would mean *gewoon meisje*) but a vulgar girl, and so on.

Don't mimic the Dutch

Although expats fall prey to Dunglish, the worst offenders are the Dutch themselves. So much English has crept into their own language that they are constantly being tripped up by Anglo-Saxon-sounding words when they try to switch to 'real' English. For this reason alone, it is always safer for the Dutch to learn English from a native than from a fellow countryman.

One annoying mistake which Dutch speakers have passed on to each other is worth dwelling on. It is the incorrect pronunciation of 'sparring partner'.

For some inexplicable reason, the Dutch pronounce 'sparring' as 'sparing' (as if the word should rhyme with 'spare ribs' instead of with the European supermarket chain Spar). This mistake has been passed on and repeated so often that the incorrect pronunciation has now become dominant. Indeed, the word is pronounced so consistently wrong that you'd almost feel embarrassed if you used it correctly in Dutch company. The Dutch will think that you are making a mistake, whereas the English speakers will immediately understand what you mean.

The mystery surrounding 'sparring partner' is intriguing. English is of course a terrible language to pronounce and to spell because of all the inconsistencies you need to recognize and then memorize. But this is not the case with 'sparring'. The double 'rr' in the middle of the word calls for a short 'a', not the longer 'ea' sound which Dutch speakers have added for some reason.

The example of 'sparring partners' but also of other common mistakes (welcome 'in', for example, or the misspelled term wishfull thinking) is a reminder that English and English idioms are best learned from native speakers themselves.

Most of all, however, Dutch speakers should look to native speakers for instruction in the subtle but oh-so-important cultural components of English. Learning vocabulary and studying grammar will not get you to your final destination – native (or near-native) English. Speaking the language properly requires, as we have seen, an appreciation for the native's own attitude to his or her language, insights into politeness and deference, and even the adoption of a new way of looking at numbers, weights and measures.

Learning to speak native English is nothing if not an adventure. Along the way there are pitfalls – think of verb tenses and especially the present continuous – but also rewards. No guide book can ever hope to take the place of the trip itself. Your journey into native English can only be accomplished by plunging into the language with your eyes wide open to both the pleasures and frustrations of this exasperating yet inspiring language.